The Irish Texans

John Brendan Flannery

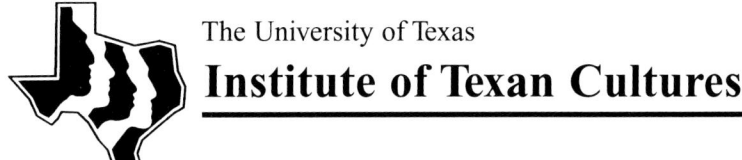

The University of Texas
Institute of Texan Cultures

The Irish Texans

John Brendan Flannery

The Irish Texans
by John Brendan Flannery

Second, revised edition

Copyright © 1995
The University of Texas Institute of Texan Cultures
801 South Bowie Street, San Antonio, Texas 78205-3296

Rex H. Ball, Executive Director
Carey Deckard, Director of Production

Design of 1980 edition by John E. Johnson
ITC Production Staff for 1995 edition: Sandra Hodsdon Carr, editor;
  James G. Cosgrove, designer; and Thomas Shelton, photographic researcher

Library of Congress Catalog Card Number 79-89957
International Standard Book Number 0-86701-071-1

All rights reserved

This publication has been made possible, in part, by a grant from
  The Houston Endowment, Inc.

Printed in the United States of America

Contents

Foreword 1
San Jacinto 7
Why Were They Here? 13
An Irish Conquistador and Others 15
Irish Mexicans 21
The "Non-Irish" Colonies 25
The Irish Empresarios 29
The San Patricio Colony 35
The Refugio Colony 41
Everyday Life in the Colonies 47
Two Would-be Towns and
   a Texas Frontier Storekeeper 57
Pro-Mexican Irish? 63
The First Skirmishes 69
The Santa Anna Campaign 73
None Paid a Greater Price 77
The Irish of Victoria 89
Disturbances in the Irish Colonies, 1835-1852 95
Texas Irish and the Civil War 97
The Irish of San Antonio 101
The Irish of the Corpus Christi Area 107
The Liberty-Beaumont Areas 117
Irish Railroaders and Houston-Galveston 121
All of God's Children 127
Honorable Mention 133
Not All Wore White Hats 137
In Conclusion 141
About the Author 144
Acknowledgments 145
Sources 146
Unpublished Manuscripts 148
Family Records 148
Notes 149
Photographic Credits 160
Index 163

Foreword

The history of the Irish in Texas parallels that of the state. Although heavy concentrations of this Celtic people appeared in certain areas of early Texas such as Staggers Point, west of the Guadalupe River, and in towns like San Antonio, Corpus Christi, Refugio, and Houston, they left their imprint on the whole state.

Their special contributions have sometimes passed unnoticed because of their very numbers and the fact that they are often classified as Anglo-Saxon or Anglo-American. Some authors refer to them as English, probably because, in the 18th and early 19th centuries, all sailings of the Irish for America originated at English ports. Another possible explanation may be found in the English Act of Union of 1800 which declared Ireland, Scotland, and Wales to be one nation with England—a union the Celtic Irish never recognized and continued to resist until they gained independence in 1921.

While any pure racial strains may have long since ceased to exist, the Irish can properly claim, with the Highland Scots, Welsh, and inhabitants of Brittany, that they represent the survival of an ethnic group that once dominated Europe—the Celts. Their language, customs, traditions, and history are Celtic. This heritage has, throughout history, reinforced their identity as a people. It had done so for more than a thousand years before Anglo-Saxonism originated in England in the melding of those two Germanic peoples with others already there. The strength and resilience of Celtic culture explain two other points in

Ireland in 1824

this account that may cause controversy: the claiming as Irish of those of Irish birth with obviously non-Irish names and of those with Irish names who were not born in Ireland.

The Irish have always absorbed and molded to the Irish image those who came to live among them. Such newcomers became identified with Ireland, her history, and her culture. Ireland had a rich tradition and culture that absorbed newcomers. Their names became Celticized, and, in the complaint of the English Lord Asquith, "they became more Irish than the Irish themselves." Jews, for example, were not easily absorbed by most other nations, but in Ireland they became "Irish," identifying with the Irish and their struggle for political and national freedom. Even Vikings became "Irish." Today's name Dillon is considered Irish, but dates back to the Viking raiders of the 7th and 8th centuries who established a settlement that later became Dublin. Names like Power (de Poer), Burke (de Burgo), and Fitzgerald date to Anglo-Norman times. The 12th century Normans were absorbed and Celticised with amazing speed and thoroughness. The process of absorption has continued to modern times—much to the dismay of the conquering English. Many of Ireland's latter-day national heroes bear names like Tone, Emmet, Davis, Parnell, and Griffith. Thus, anyone born in Ireland or immediately involved in any part of the Irish experience is considered Irish.

That which gave cohesion and identification to the Irish in Ireland was not a political system. Their political history is, in fact, one of fragmentation and disunity. Even so, they recognized a shared culture, language, social and tribal system, legal system, mythology, literature, and even pagan religious roots—all distinctly Celtic and Irish. Since their commonality was not a national political system, it bound the Irish throughout the world in a sense of sharing something unique that transcends nationalism.

The bearer of an Irish name or descent may know nothing of his forebears' history or of his heritage, but he does know that he is one with a people distinct and apart from others. That "Irish identity" is preserved wherever the Irish go, and the awareness of it is handed down to later generations. In Texas today, among the descendants of the 1830's Irish pioneers, one finds that same strong identification with the Irish heritage. Thus, anyone who bears an ancient Celtic surname can call himself "Irish."

One final reminder to the reader who is not familiar with Texas history: Texas was settled, revolution was carried out, and the frontiers were explored by handfuls of determined men. Populations were smaller then. Many ethnic groups and nationalities were represented, and all Texans have reason to be proud. In 1835 the population of the province was about 30,000—and those were sharply divided on the issue of independence. Up to and at the time of the Battle of San Jacinto, the Texas army was counted in the hundreds, and most were citizen-soldiers.

But there were Irish Mexicans by political adoption before this revolution, and many an Irish settler long after. Small as the early numbers were, this is only the story of examples of Irish participation in Texas's settlement, independence, and development up to the turn of the 20th century. Irish descendants are now legion, and a book listing "everyone" or bestowing contemporary honors is not the purpose here.

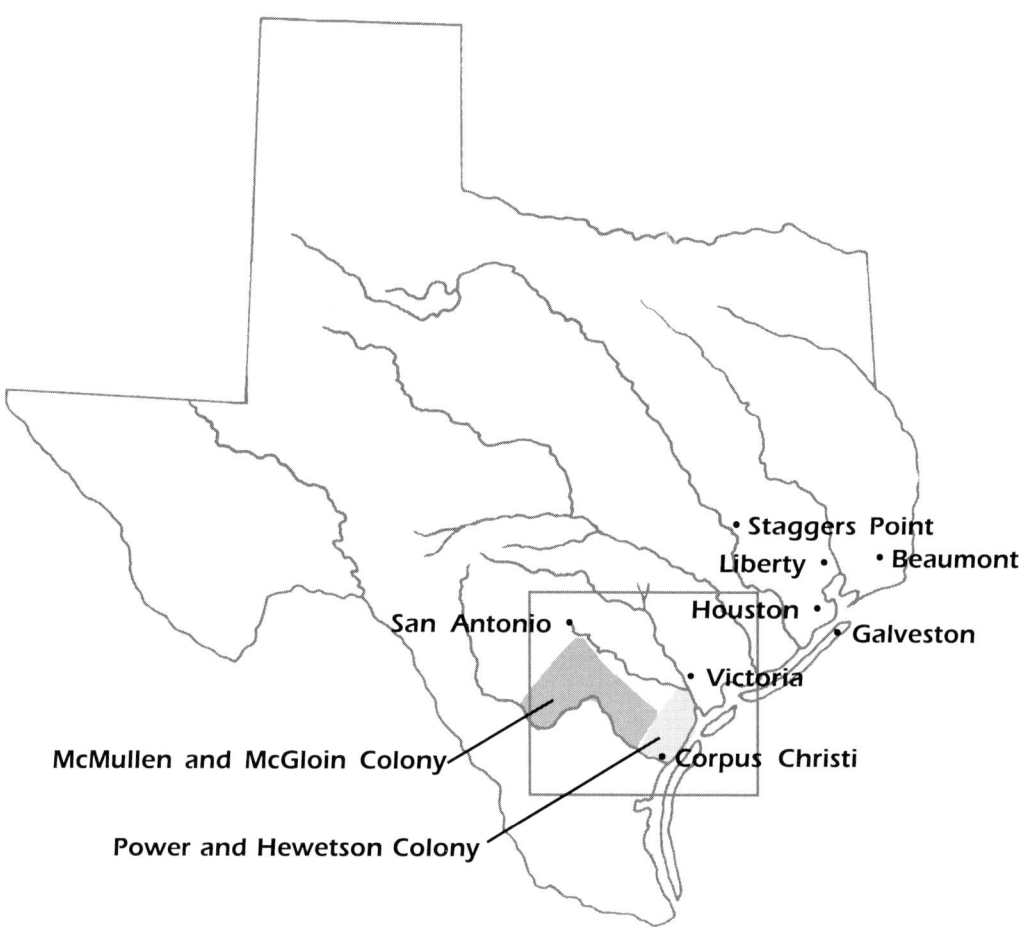

The Irish colonies and other areas of Irish settlement

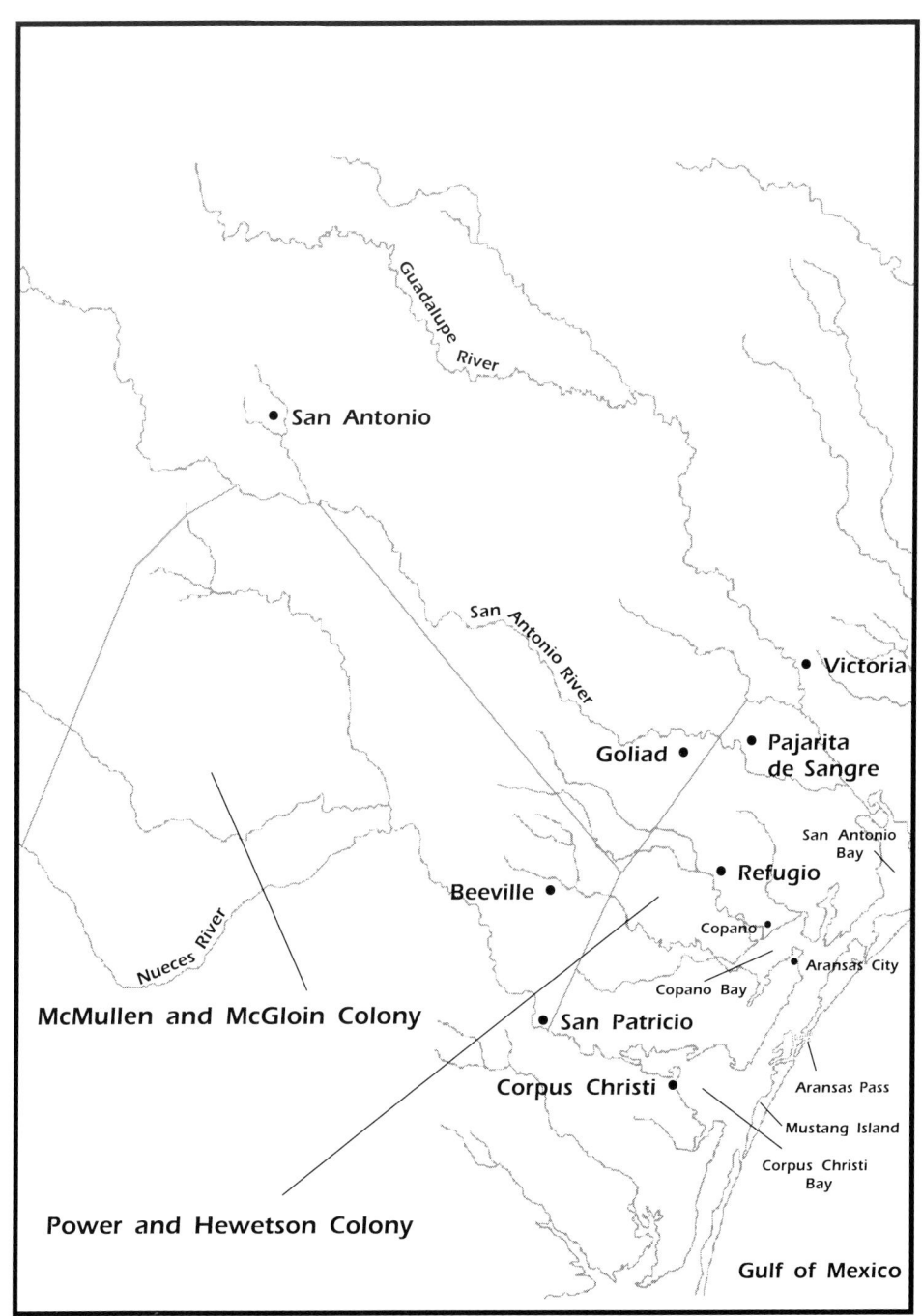

San Jacinto

As battles go, San Jacinto was a small one. There were no massed thousands on either side, no great artillery duels, and only one mounted charge. The opposing armies met, and the issue was decided—in 18 minutes—on a few acres of ground in what was known locally as "the McCormick League." Yet many historians rank that short, bloody conflict with Arbela, Tours, Saratoga, and Waterloo as one of the decisive battles that forever changed history. The very place-names—Buffalo Bayou and San Jacinto River—identify the conflict between an advancing new American frontier and an established order of European derivation.

Such considerations were far from the thoughts of the soldiers gathered there on the evening of April 21, 1836. Some, oblivious to the heaps of Mexican dead, succumbed to postbattle weariness—a mixture of relief and thankfulness for survival. Others, brandishing the long rifles that had proved so devastating, were busy herding prisoners. Propped against a tree directing all the hubbub was the injured general, Sam Houston, his ankle shattered by a rifleball.

For days afterward, hot sunshine alternated with periods of rain, and some six hundred enemy corpses lay unburied on the battlefield. In spite of the unbearable stench, the wounded and feverish general remained at the site, eager to exploit his victory and stem the panicked flight of Texas families. Until he was moved on May 1, his makeshift headquarters managed both official business—especially after the capture of Santa Anna—and unofficial activities, for the plain of St. Hyacinth had immediately become a tourist attraction.

The marsh on the McCormick property which prevented the escape of the retreating Mexican army

A few days after the battle, Mrs. Peggy McCormick came galloping into the field and headed straight for General Houston, who was surrounded by subordinates, couriers, and scouts. Exhibiting the frontiersman's deference for women, the men fell silent at her approach and cleared a path. She reined in her horse a few feet from the general and addressed him with an agitation that gave emphasis to her Irish brogue, curtly requesting him to remove the "stinking corpses" from her land.

Sam Houston regarded the distraught woman. The decomposing bodies had indeed concerned him; he had even discussed the matter with Santa Anna, yet nothing had been accomplished so far. Irish colonist John J. Linn, who was among those delivering supplies to the camp, records Houston's polite but patronizing response:

"Madam, your land will be famed in history as the classic spot upon which the glorious victory of San Jacinto was gained! Here was born, in the throes of revolution, and amid the strife of contending legions, the infant of Texan independence! Here that latest scourge of mankind, the arrogantly self-styled 'Napoleon of the West' met his fate!"

"To the devil with your glorious history!" answered the impatient Irishwoman, then, wheeling her horse, she roughly demanded that Houston remove the corpses and galloped off.[1]

Peggy McCormick personified that sudden practicality of Irish womanhood that has always acted as a moderating influence on the rash and impetuous idealism of the men. She and her husband, an Irish barrister, had left Ireland in 1822 and had taken up land on the Texas coast near the present city of Houston. Her husband, Arthur, drowned in the San Jacinto River in 1832, and Peggy McCormick was left alone to raise two young sons and operate a ranch. She proved herself a strong-willed woman.

On April 16, 1836, a few days prior to San Jacinto, her son Michael had been dispatched by General Houston to New Washington to warn the Texas president, David G. Burnet, and his cabinet of the approach of the Mexican army. On the way Michael discovered an advance party of 50 dragoons under Colonel Juan N. Almonte riding hard for the town. Putting spurs to his horse, he outdistanced the Mexican detachment and rode into New Washington minutes ahead of them. There he found Burnet haggling with the ferry operator about transport. At McCormick's shouted warning, Burnet jumped into the rowboat, which immediately put out from shore. The young messenger spurred his horse into the brush as the frustrated Mexicans dashed to the river bank. Several leveled their guns at the receding rowboat, but Almonte forbade their shooting because a woman, Mrs. Burnet, was in the boat.[2]

The McCormicks were not the only Irish, nor the first, to be associated with Texas and its history. Irish have been a part of Texas from Spanish times to the present. They came as soldiers and statesmen in Spanish service; they came as

The Battle of San Jacinto, *by Irish-born Harry Arthur McArdle, completed in 1895. In order to create an authoritative record of the battle, McArdle interviewed survivors and located uniforms, equipment, and portraits of participants. Detail below shows Sam Houston (lower right) waving his hat as he prepares to lead his men on foot.*

colonials under Mexican law; and no group paid a higher price for Texas independence than did the Irish colonies west of the Guadalupe River. Their men fought and fell at the Alamo, Goliad, San Patricio, Agua Dulce Creek, Coleto Creek, and Refugio. Their homes, land, and livestock were raided and laid waste by Mexican and Texan armies. What was left was pillaged by marauding bands of Indians, Mexican brigands, and American freebooters. But the Irish-Texan story began long before this.

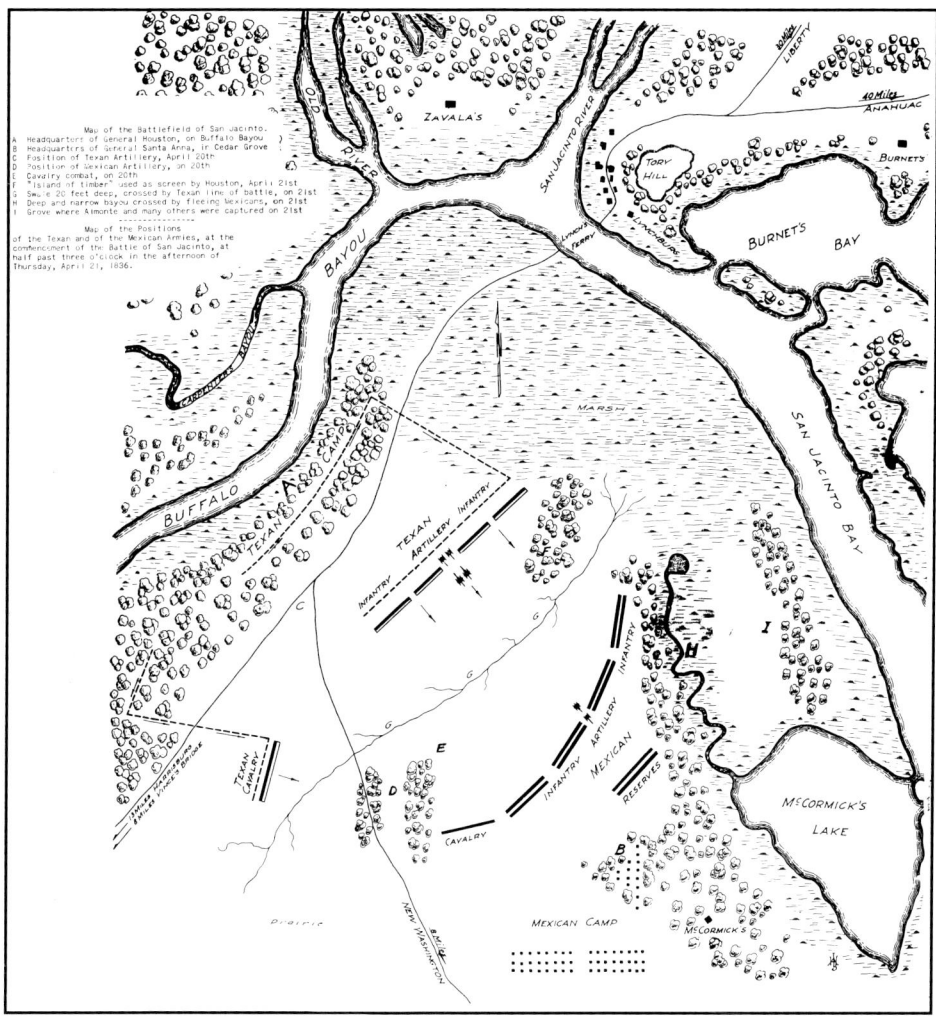

San Jacinto battlefield; Peggy McCormick's house (lower right) *near McCormick's Lake*

Survivors of earlier engagements were with General Houston at San Jacinto. Among them were Irish-born William McGuill, William Redmond, Walter Lambert, Thomas O'Connor, James O'Connor, Charles Malone, Edmund Quirk, Martin O'Toole, William Cassidy, and Daniel O'Driscoll of the Irish colonies west of the Guadalupe River and Robert Henry, Edward McMillan, Benjamin Bryant, and Matthew Dunn of the Scots Irish of Staggers Point near the Brazos River.[3] In all, about a hundred Irish-born men participated in the Battle of San Jacinto, making up about one-seventh of the Texas army.

Why Were They Here?

The Irish presence in Texas was part of a long stream of emigration that started with the English defeat of Irish armies at the Battle of Kinsale, Ireland, in 1602. It slackened only with the attainment of Irish independence 320 years later. The Irish were robbed of their ancestral lands, denied education, and prohibited from holding office or having political representation. They were persecuted for their religion and forbidden their age-old culture and legal system. They were reduced to that state so aptly described by an English Lord Chancellor and Lord Chief Justice of the late 18th century: "No such person as an Irish Catholic is presumed to exist under English law." [1]

Generation after generation rose in futile, and disunited, opposition to English rule. After each defeat new bands of emigrants headed for France, Spain, Austria—any nation that was at war with England. Some of these and their descendants came to New Spain and Texas. They were sometimes listed on immigration roles as natives of their adopted countries.

When the English king, William of Orange, defeated the Irish at the Boyne River in 1690, the government appropriated the lands of the northern Celtic Irish and parceled them out to Scottish Lowlanders of William's army. These were principally Presbyterians. Those of the dispossessed Irish who were not shipped to the Carolinas or West Indies were allowed to stay on their ancestral lands as menials, providing cheap labor. Thus, by a national policy 300 years ago, England created in Northern Ireland a situation that pitted "haves" against "have nots" and religion against religion. Some of the fruits are still being reaped in Northern Ireland today. The Scottish "planters," while they sought to preserve their economic advantage, identified with the country like all who had come to Ireland before and came to be known as "Scots Irish."

Initially, as Protestants, the Presbyterian, or Scots, Irish enjoyed certain economic rights denied to the Catholic Irish.[2] However, during the 18th century, they suffered equally with Catholics from the rapaciousness of landlords and from England's mercantilist policies.[3] Also, like the Catholics, they were forced to pay tithes for the support of the Anglican Church to which they did not belong.

In 1703 England passed the Test Act. This act required all officeholders in Ireland to conform to the "established," or Anglican, Church. The Presbyterian Irish saw in this an extension to them of the discrimination already legislated against the Catholic Irish.[4] England's "choking off" of the developing woolen trade and the discriminatory English Corn Laws further alienated that segment of the Irish. As a consequence, more than 250,000 individuals immigrated to the American colonies between 1717 and the Revolutionary War. [5]

In Ireland common cause brought Catholics and Protestants together in a political movement of the late 18th century known as "The United Irishmen." The goal was an Irish republic, and the result was the 1798 Uprising. It was bloodily put down by the English with the aid of Hessian mercenaries. The brutal reprisals thereafter visited upon a helpless citizenry increased the stream of emigration.[6]

In the 19th century, England's unchanged mercantilist policies continued to feed that stream. The Irish saw no future in a land where, as in the 1840's, their livestock and grain was being shipped to England, while millions of Irish died from starvation due to the failure of the potato crop.[7] They continued to be second-class citizens in their own land. Advancement for even the learned and professional depended upon their support of a governmental system dedicated to the abolition of the only thing left to them—their identity as a people. Little wonder that families scrimped and saved to send their bright young people to places like Texas where opportunity beckoned.

An Irish Conquistador and Others

While the area of the New World now known as Texas was under Spanish rule, the Irish were here as soldiers, administrators, priests, and settlers. They remained when Mexico obtained its independence, and some helped shape Mexican history.

A rigorous dedication to the service of his king and adopted country broke the health of an 18th century conquistador known to the Indians, because of his red hair, as "Capitán Colorado." Hugh O'Connor was born in Dublin in 1734 but later, running afoul of the English, fled to Spain. He entered the military and became an officer in the Volunteer Regiment of Aragon. Service in Cuba was followed by assignment to New Spain, of which Texas was a part. In Spanish his name became Hugo Oconór, and his appointments increased in rank. He came to Texas in 1767 and served as governor from that year to 1770.[1] In 1768 he participated in the laying of the first stones for the walls of the church at Mission San José y San Miguel de Aguayo in San Antonio.[2]

Beginning in the late 1600's, the Apache Indians had carried on unrelenting warfare against Spanish settlements. Their attacks increased in frequency and ferocity during the 18th century as they were driven from their hunting grounds by the more powerful Comanches. Spanish officials estimated that, between 1748 and 1772, the Apaches killed more than 4,000 persons and stole or destroyed property valued at over 12 million pesos.[3]

Mission San José, San Antonio, 1860's. Hugo Oconór and Fray Gaspar José de Solís, guardian of the college at Zacatecas, laid the first stones for the walls of this church during ceremonies held on March 19, 1768.

The estimates were probably high, but the trouble was constant. Spanish garrisons were undermanned, and there was no uniform policy for dealing with the Indians. Some local commanders fought them, while others tried to pacify them with gifts and treaties. The missionaries tried to teach them peaceful pursuits, Christianize them, and induce them to settle on the land. Compared with the small successes the padres had with some Indian groups, however, they had practically no influence on the Apaches.

Garrison soldiers were poorly armed and poorly mounted. Morale was low in some presidios. Enlisted men were often even in debt to their commanders, who at times made questionable deductions from their pay. An inspection of Texas settlements and garrisons in 1767 disclosed glaring weaknesses in defense. San Antonio, the most important Spanish settlement in Texas, was defended by as few as 22 soldiers, and some of these spent their time away from town guarding five nearby missions. Several times even the horses of the presidio were stolen by Indians. Time and again, ranchers were driven from their lands, and, when the Apaches were on the prowl, none dared leave the security of town or mission except in large groups. Lone horsemen or small groups were often captured or killed. These were the conditions facing Colonel Hugo Oconór when, in 1772, he was made *comandante inspector*, directly

Presidio La Bahía, Goliad, 1890's. In 1772 Hugo Oconór became comandante inspector *over this presidio and all others in the northern provinces of Mexico.*

responsible to the viceroy and charged with bringing order and security to the northern frontier of New Spain, which extended from Texas to California.

Abandoning some of the less-defensible positions, he formed a defense line with the 22 presidios extending from La Bahía at Goliad in Texas to Santa Gertrudis de Altar in Sonora near the Gulf of California—a distance of 1,500 miles. These he manned with 2,300 men, assigning regular patrols. This thin defensive line was to put a stop to the Indian raids into Mexico. Meanwhile, he mounted an offensive campaign that drove back the Apaches.

Oconór's reorganization of the frontier garrisons involved establishing standards of arms, dress, mounts, and proficiency of the soldier. Commanders were forbidden to buy and sell supplies to the troops. Salaries were set for all ranks, and a paymaster was made responsible for finances and the procurement of supplies. The duties and responsibilities of each rank were specified, and a promotional system based on merit was inaugurated. [4]

Within four years this dedicated Irishman had brought relative peace and security to the frontier of New Spain. However, the responsibilities of his administration and the rigors of Indian campaigns, which he occasionally would lead personally, left him broken in health. Oconór was transferred from his frontier duty and died at age 45 while serving as governor of Yucatán.

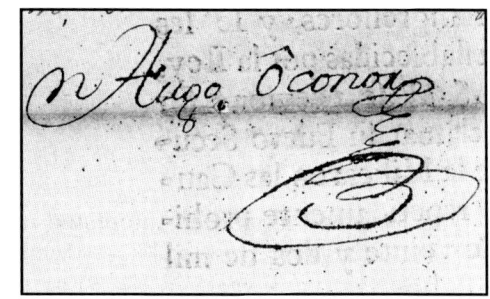

Signature of Hugo Oconór, July 22, 1768

Oconór was not the only Irishman to undergo a name change to adapt to the pronunciation of a foreign language. In Spain O'Donoghue became O'Donojú, and Murphy became Morphy or Morfi.

One of the latter, Juan Agustín Morfi, priest and historian, faithfully recorded life as he saw it in New Spain. In 1777 he accompanied Comandante General de Croix on his tour of the provinces, making notes for his *Viaje de Indios*. He visited Texas and later wrote a history of the area. Not much escaped the good padre's keen eye, and he did not hesitate to record a couple of incidents of some embarrassment to himself. Father Morfi was apparently an avid fisherman, but poor weather and official business had kept him from this sport when he first came to San Antonio. Finally, with a break in the weather, he and two of de Croix's officers decided to try their luck in the San Antonio River. They were crossing the plaza ankle-deep in mud when they were startled by a sound from behind. A bull was loose in the plaza and seemed determined to occupy the area alone. He charged and, self-preservation taking precedence over sport for the day, the three men ran for their lives despite the mud. Misfortune seemed to attend Father Morfi's attempts at fishing—at least in the Texas area. On the return trip to Mexico, he stopped to fish in the Rio Grande, but, through unexplained circumstances, fell in![5] He was apparently an indifferent angler, but there can be no doubt of his superior ability as a chronicler. Modern historians owe much to him for his objective account of life in those times.

There were other Irish in Texas during Spanish times. The censuses of Nacogdoches, on the eastern border, record many Irish-born Spanish subjects. The 1792 census indicates that Philip Nolan of Belfast was one of the first. Other sources show that James Conilt was there in 1786.[6] This may be the same man listed in the 1801 records as James Maconilt. Other 18th century listings of Irish-born men are: Richard Sims and William Barr in 1793; Francisco Cornegay, 1794; Thomas Blain, 1796; and James McNulty "of Munster" in 1797. Between the years 1801 and 1806, the census records show seven other Irishmen as Spanish subjects. One of these is listed as John Oconór, "native of the capital of Connaught." The references to Munster and Connaught, Irish provinces, are unusual. An Irishman generally identifies himself by the county from which he came rather than the province.

Since Louisiana was under Spanish domination during the latter part of the 18th century, entry of foreign settlers to Texas from the east was easy. Once in Louisiana, they were only a step from Texas. Most who came to Nacogdoches entered from the former French colony.

The Irish had long been interested in settlement in Lousiana. In 1787 a Virginian, Bryan Browin, requested permission to bring 12 wealthy Irish families to that area. In that year a William Fitzgerald was allowed a 1,000 peso advance to transport 30 Irish families from New York. An Irishman, retired French army officer Augustine MacArty (McCarthy), offered to induce two to three thousand Irish Catholics to settle in Louisiana.[7] It is impossible to ascertain the number of Irish that came to Louisiana as a result of these efforts, but there was considerable Irish emigration from the United States. Some of these drifted west into Texas.

In 1806 plans went forward for the founding in Texas of a town on the Trinity River west of Nacogdoches. It was to be named Villa de Santísima Trinidad de Salcedo. Founders came from Louisiana and Béxar (San Antonio). Some Irish were already there when, in January of 1807, 16 persons arrived from Béxar.[8]

Among the Irish at Villa de Santísima Trinidad de Salcedo were: Miguel Quinn, Juan Magee and family, Enrique Seridan (Sheridan), the family of Juan Lunn, Hugo Coyle,[9] James Fear and family, and John Mulroney.[10] In 1809 new settlers appearing at Salcedo were Patricio Fitzgerald and Timoteo Barrett of Ireland.[11] Zebulon Pike, in his *Journals*, mentions reaching the Trinity River in Texas (probably at Salcedo), and meeting, among others, a number of Irishmen.

Irish Mexicans

Mexico records many Irish names in its political, religious, and intellectual life. Two such names are Obregon (O'Brien) and Barragan (Berrigan). In the early 1800's, an Ignacio Obregon is listed as one of many large landowners protesting a Spanish law that threatened the Mexican economy.[1] Joaquin Obregon headed the Finance and Commerce Committee of Agustín de Iturbide's cabinet after 1821. Obregons were later prominent in Mexican politics—one of them a president of the republic.

General Miguel Barragan served as interim president of Mexico under Santa Anna. A Captain Marcos Barragan was with Santa Anna's army in Texas in 1836; escaping from San Jacinto, he brought news of the defeat to General José de Urrea.[2] General Juan O'Donojú (O'Donoghue) served as the last viceroy to New Spain in 1821 and affirmed Mexican independence. His chaplain, Father Miguel Muldoon, is of special interest to Texas because of his involvement with the Austin colonists.

Father Muldoon was the son of an Irishman who fled to Spain and there married a Spanish girl. Muldoon entered the priesthood in Spain, but a love of adventure caused him to ask for assignment in the New World. On arrival in Mexico, he asked to be assigned to the frontier. Eventually he was assigned to Stephen F. Austin's colony and seemed to adapt readily to frontier conditions. Muldoon, apparently of a friendly nature and jovial disposition, got along well with the Anglo-American colonists, most of whom were Protestants, although

General Juan O'Donojú, the last Spanish viceroy before Mexican independence

they had professed Catholicism in order to enter Spanish Texas. They looked forward to his scheduled visits for baptisms and weddings. He enlivened such festive events by his wit and ready humor and had the ability to compose, on the spot, poetry to fit the occasion. The toast he gave on January 1, 1832, at a banquet honoring Stephen F. Austin, is one example and conveys something of the personal philosophy of the man.

Father Muldoon's Toast:

> May plow and harrow, spade and fack
> Remain the arms of Anahuac
> So that her rich and boundless plains
> May yearly yield all sorts of grains.
> May all religious discord fall
> And friendship be the creed of all.
> With tolerance your pastor views
> All sects of Christians, Turks, and Jews.
> We now demand three rousing cheers
> Great Austin's health and pioneers. [3]

Marker honoring Father Miguel Muldoon, Fayette County

Father Muldoon rendered invaluable aid to the early colonists in their controversies with Mexican officialdom. In 1832 he and Thomas Jefferson Chambers helped the colonists draft, in Spanish, their protests against the newly established customshouse at Anahuac. On Trinity Bay east of the present city of Houston, Anahuac was a required port of entry for colonists and supplies. The settlers objected to customs regulations and fees.

There was no question of Muldoon's personal courage. Some colonists had been imprisoned at Anahuac following their protest, and he accompanied their angry neighbors, who marched to their aid. To prevent bloodshed, he attempted conciliation with the Mexican commander and, failing, offered himself as a hostage for the prisoners.[4] At another time he went alone to an Indian camp and secured the release of a captive white woman.

In 1834 Stephen F. Austin was in prison in Mexico City suspected of supporting revolution. Father Muldoon visited him there, bringing food and books and giving what aid and comfort he could.[5] Later, without regard for his own safety, he aided William H. Wharton in escaping from prison at Matamoros, Mexico. Wharton had been captured at sea by the Mexican navy on his return to Texas from the United States, where he had been lobbying in support of annexation. Muldoon apparently had great sympathy for the Texas cause.

Today one hears the Texas term "Muldoon Catholic" applied to one whose Catholicism is only a veneer. It was used in frontier days for those members of Father Muldoon's flock who, originally Protestant, professed Catholicism only to secure Mexican lands in Texas. The conditions of frontier life, the distances to be traveled, and the lack of educational facilities prompted a rather pragmatic approach on Father Muldoon's part in accepting and certifying as "Catholic" those whose conversions were superficial. It is not a criticism of his personal faith.

Father Muldoon earned the love and respect of the Texans who knew him.[6] Before he left Texas he received from President Sam Houston, in behalf of the people of Texas, a letter thanking him for the services he had rendered. A town in Fayette County was named in his memory, and on Highway 77, south of the town of La Grange, stands a memorial erected to the memory of this "Forgotten man of Texas history."

The "Non-Irish" Colonies

The Irish in Texas are often thought of in terms of the so-called "Irish colonists" of San Patricio and Refugio. They were the most noticeable Texas Irish. However, there were Irish who had come from the United States to the Austin, De León, Peters, DeWitt, and Robertson colonies, and to the eastern part of the state near the Louisiana border. Most of them came to the province of Texas because of the availability of inexpensive land.

The high purchase price ($2.00 per acre) of public lands in the United States prior to 1820 forced many homesteaders to finance their purchases through local state banks using the land as security. In 1818 there were mass failures of those banks in the West and South. Many individuals lost their lands, put signs on their property saying "GTT" (Gone to Texas), and headed for Mexico. A league of land (about 4,428 acres) could be had for just homesteading, or paying a surveyor's fee, or for at most about $100. The unemployment in the northern cities in the 1819-1820 depression also caused some migration from those areas. The price of United States public lands dropped to $1.25 per acre after 1820, but payment was to be in cash, and severe depression again struck in 1837. Farmers moved on once more, seeking cheaper lands.

Stephen F. Austin's Old Three Hundred, the settlers of his first colony, included Irish-born members, among them Martin Allen, Arthur and Peggy McCormick, and Alexander and Humphrey Jackson. Listed also are: Callaghan, Clark, Cummings, Fitzgerald, Hughes, Kennedy, Kelly, Lynch, Moore, and another McCormick.[1] Even before Austin had selected the land for his colony, two Irish families, Garrett and Higgins, were in the area. In December of 1821, they were said to have built cabins two miles above the mouth of the Little Brazos River.[2]

Early education in Austin's colony appeared to be in the hands of the Irish. M.M. Kenney, in his "Recollections of Early Schools," notes that, in the years 1835 to 1840, the schoolteachers were Irishmen. One of those teachers was so well-liked by the community, and he in turn so enjoyed his position as a teacher, that plans were made to open an academy. He sailed from New Orleans for Ireland to bring his family back to Texas. However, the vessel was lost with all aboard. Such peril was common at the time. Later in 1842, another teacher, named Cummins, volunteered for the Texas army to join in fighting off a Mexican attack on San Antonio. He was killed at the Battle of Salado Creek.[3]

The Mexican colonizer Martín de León had invited Irish settlers into his colony in the area of Victoria. Perhaps the most famous arrival was John J. Linn, whose college-professor father had to flee Ireland for his part in the 1798 Uprising. Linn went to New Orleans in 1822 and established a trading business. An illicit trade between Americans and Mexicans of the Texas river towns had sprung up in the late 1820's. Linn, dealing in tobacco, was part of this trade. He became interested in Texas and settled in de León's colony. Other Irish settlers there included Patrick Mahan and James Quinn.

In 1821 eight Irish families came from northern Ireland to South Carolina; after some time there, they moved to Alabama. Between 1829 and 1834, they immigrated to Texas, settling in a wooded section west of the present town of Benchley in Robertson County. The community became known as Staggers Point, the name deriving from "striver," indicating a determination to succeed.[4] Staggers Point was a "thriving Irish town" by the time of the Texas Revolution.

The Original Irish Settlers of Staggers Point

William Henry, Mary Fullerton Henry Dixon, James M. Dixon, Ann McMillan, Henry and Sarah Fullerton, Robert and Elizabeth Henry, George H. Fullerton, John R. and Sarah Payton, Jimmie H. Rice, William Fullerton, Hugh and Elizabeth Henry, James A. Henry, Bradford and Mary Henry Seale, James and Isabella Dunn, and Columbus and Elizabeth Henry Seale.[5]

The settlers lost no time in putting down roots in the land. James Dunn built a fort to which the colonists repaired when Indians threatened. Devout Presbyterians, they erected what became known as the Old Irish Church on Red Top Prairie.

The community was constantly harassed by Indians. New Year's Day of 1839, a time of new beginnings and new hope, was a tragic time for the George

Store and public scales, Benchley, c. 1892. Scots-Irish Presbyterians founded the nearby community of Staggers Point in 1833. After the railroad bypassed their settlement in 1868, the colony relocated and named the new community after railroad conductor Henry W. Benchley.

Morgan family. Indians plundered the home, killing several members of the family. Nine days later 70 warriors attacked another settler's home. Meanwhile, after burying the dead of the Morgan massacre, 48 men had organized under Benjamin Bryant to hunt down the Indians. In a battle known locally as Bryant's Defeat, the settlers suffered severe losses.

Confident in their numbers and convinced that their quarry was hidden in some woods ahead, the settlers advanced across the prairie in an extended line. Suddenly, with blood-chilling war whoops, a large body of Indians charged from the cover of the woods. In the din of Indian war cries, Bryant's shouted commands were unheard by his men. Horses and men went down in a shower of arrows. Except for a few close enough to fight back-to-back, each man was cut off from the others, and all fought desperate hand-to-hand combat. Some escaped, but among the dead were Bryant and ten of the Staggers Point Irish.

The Peters Colony of the 1840's was located in the northern part of the state, south of the Red River boundary with Oklahoma and in the general area of the present city of Dallas. It covered the present Texas counties of Montague, Wise, Cooke, Grayson, Denton, Collin, and parts of Parker, Tarrant, Dallas, and Johnson counties between the Brazos and the Trinity rivers. There were 87 Irish-surnamed colonists among the settlers, although biographical sketches note that only five were born in Ireland.[6]

The present city of Dallas was founded by John N. Bryan who, in 1841, came to the area and built a cabin on the east bank of the Trinity River near what is now the courthouse square. He laid out a townsite and apparently publicized it widely, since it appears on early Peters Colony maps and was known in the United States. It was visited by a Missourian in 1844, who disappointedly wrote: "We soon reached the place we had heard of so often; but the town, where was it? Two small log cabins—this was the town of Dallas, and two families of 10 or 12 souls was its population."[7]

Irish Surnamed of the Peters Colony

Joseph Boyle, Catherine Brien, John N. Bryan, Stephen W. Callaghan, Harvey Casey, John Casey, John Casey Jr., John Casey Sr., Thomas Casey, Timothy Casey, Thomas Cassidy, Thomas Cassidy Sr., Elisha C. Clary, Elisha T. Clary, Albert G. Collins, John H. Collins, Thomas Collins, Cornelius Conely, William D. Conner, Joseph W. Connor, John Conway, Hugh Coween, Dan Delaney, George W. Dooley, James Dooley, William Dooley, William Gallagher, Abraham Hart, Caleb Hart, Jacob Hart, William J. Hart, Daniel B. Hearn, Martin Hearn, William A. Hearn, John Higgins, Lewis T. Higgins, Philemon Higgins, William Higgins, Thomas Keenan, Calvin W. Kennedy, James Kennedy, John Kennedy, Mary Kennedy, Samuel Kennedy, Arthur Kerrigan, James P. Laughlin, Newton C. Laughlin, William B. Laughlin, James McBride, Gerard McCarty, Larkin McCarty, William McCarty Jr., William McCarty Sr., Patrick McClary, Joseph B. McDermott, John C. McElroy, J. McNamara, Thomas Mahan, Perry Malone, John Maloney, Charles Manihan, Delilah C. Manning, John Manning, Eli Murphy, Henderson Murphy, Thomas G. Murphy, Ambrose R. Murray, Daniel Murray, Christopher Nolan, John O'Hara, William O'Neal, Martin O'Neil, Leonida O'Quinn, Stephen O'Quinn, William O'Quinn, George W. Ragan, William M. Roark, James R. Rylie, Benjamin Shahan, Daniel Shahan, Elizabeth Shahan, William P. Shahan, Andrew Shannon, Robert E. Shannon, and James Sullivan.[8]

The Irish Empresarios

Four Irishmen founded the two Texas settlements known as the San Patricio and the Refugio colonies. Although the settlers were mainly Irish, there were Mexicans and other nationalities in each area. The settlement of John McMullen and James McGloin was known as the San Patricio Colony; that of James Power and James Hewetson, the Refugio Colony.

A "grant" to an empresario (one who contracted to settle colonists) was not an outright donation of land. It defined the area to which the empresario could bring the families he had contracted to settle. Each settler could choose his land from within the defined area—assuming it was not already legally occupied. It was then surveyed, and, if the settler met the Mexican requirements, he was confirmed in his possession and issued a title by a Mexican official named for that purpose. Each empresario had a definite time limit within which to complete his contract. Upon completion he received extensive lands for himself. Contracts, each for six years, were issued to Power and Hewetson on June 11, 1828, and to McMullen and McGloin on August 16, 1828.

James Power, born near Ballygarrett, County Wexford, Ireland, was ten years old at the time of the 1798 Uprising in Ireland. Following the Battle of Vinegar Hill fought near his home, he probably witnessed some of the carnage that ensued when the English yeomanry was turned loose on the countryside. In the years that followed, the details of that magnificent stand made by the men and women of County Wexford were often recounted around evening firesides.

What effect all this may have had on his later life is not known, but Power's enthusiastic espousal of the Texas cause was probably the reaction of one who had experienced tyranny.

At age 21 Power immigrated to Philadelphia and went from there to New Orleans, where he operated a merchandising business. Some years later he settled in Saltillo, Mexico, and became a Mexican citizen. He met Don Felipe Roque de la Portilla, who had been in charge of the attempt to organize a settlement on the San Marcos River in Texas, and probably got many ideas on colonization from him. But Power was eloquent himself—he wanted to marry Don Felipe's daughter, Dolores, so he induced the de la Portillas to move to Texas with him, and there, when he was 33, he married her. The whole family settled together on the banks of Nueces Bay near the mouth of the Nueces River.[1]

Power had teamed up with another Irishman, James Hewetson, in the colonization venture. An agent employed by them to recruit Irish settlers for their colony had been unsuccessful, and, with the empresario contract about to expire in one year, Power sailed for Ireland from Aransas Pass in April 1833.[2]

Power was successful in recruiting, but when many of the colonists were stricken by cholera in New Orleans, there was much grumbling about having been induced to come to the New World. Dissatisfaction increased when the two schooners he hired to convey them from New Orleans to Copano Bay ran aground at Aransas Pass and tools and supplies were lost. There were reports that the owners of the vessels had them heavily insured and had bribed the captains to wreck them. Some had suspicions that Power had a hand in this, but the testimony of Rosalie Hart Priour should settle that. "Colonel Power," she said, "ordered the captain of the schooner, in my presence, at the point of his pistol, to change his course and avoid running his vessel aground. . . ." The captain obeyed and anchored for the night, but ". . . in the night . . . ran our schooner ashore."[3] In spite of the troubles, the Irish settlers finally made their way to the colony.

James Power took an active part in the Texas Revolution. Although elected to the General Consultation of November 1835, he was unable to attend because he was involved in the Texan attack on the Mexican garrison at Lipantitlán on the Nueces River. He later served on the General Council, withdrawing December 29 to attend to his personal affairs.

He was elected delegate from Refugio to the Convention of March 1, 1836, and, through his influence, Sam Houston was elected second delegate. Thus, on March 2 he was one of the signers of the Texas Declaration of Independence. As a delegate to the Annexation Convention of July 4, 1845, James Power supported the annexation resolution, and when, on December 29, Texas became the 28th state, his signature was on the first State Constitution.

Power's last years were spent in costly litigation defending his title to his lands. In 1852 he became seriously ill and died on August 15 at his home on

Dr. James Hewetson, empresario

Ruins of the Power residence, Copano, 1911. This shellcrete structure was designed for James Power but was not completed until shortly after his death. His wife and a daughter lived there until it was destroyed by the hurricane of 1886.

Copano Bay. He was survived by his second wife, Tomasa de la Portilla Power, and seven children. His body was buried there at Live Oak Point, but his remains were not allowed to rest in peace. In 1873 his casket was dug up by grave robbers. The remains were removed by his family to Mount Calvary Cemetery in Refugio, where they rest today under an appropriate monument.

James Hewetson, Power's partner in the colonization project, was born in County Kilkenny, Ireland, in 1796. Sometime before 1818 he immigrated to Philadelphia. As a medical doctor, he had received what for the day was a better-than-average education. He was one of the group that, in 1821, accompanied Stephen F. Austin to Texas. The latter, as an empresario, had come here to claim the land assigned to his father by the Spanish. The group stopped in San Antonio and there learned the news of Mexico's independence from Spain. The 25-year-old Hewetson went on to Monclova, Mexico, eventually settling in Saltillo, where there were a number of Irish. He started a business in that city and met James Power there. Although he joined Power in the colonization plans, Hewetson opposed Texas independence and lived the rest of his life in Mexico, leaving to his partner the management of the colony. In 1833 he married Josefa Guajardo, a wealthy landowner.

James Hewetson witnessed, in his adopted country, the struggle between Federalism and Centralism, the loss of Texas, a war with the United States and U.S. troops as occupiers, and the many military and political power struggles that convulsed Mexico. He died on September 12, 1870, and was buried beside his wife in the Campo Santo de la Parroquia de Santiago del Saltillo.[4]

John McMullen was born in Ireland in 1785 and came with his family to Baltimore, Maryland. He later moved to Savannah, Georgia, where he married Esther Cummings in 1810. In 1825 he moved to Matamoros, Mexico, where he operated a merchandising business. Like others, he tried colonization. He and his partner and son-in-law, James McGloin, recruited the settlers for their San Patricio Colony from among Irish-born immigrants in New York and Philadelphia. They both went there for that purpose, and each accompanied one of the two vessels that brought the first colonists to Texas in 1829.

Six years later McMullen was elected one of the representatives from San Patricio to the Consultation of November 1835 and on December 11 was appointed to the General Council. He became deeply involved in the revolutionary government. On January 1, 1836, he was unanimously elected temporary president of the council. On returning to San Patricio, he saw the devastation caused by the invasion of the Mexican army and journeyed to the United States to procure supplies for the colonists. His election as a delegate to the Convention of March 1, 1836, was questioned, and he lost his seat.

He was living in San Antonio by early 1837. In March of that year, a petition was forwarded from the Catholics of San Antonio, San Patricio, Refugio, and Victoria to Bishop Blanc of New Orleans asking for English-speaking priests for

James Power's tombstone, Mount Calvary Cemetery, Refugio

James McGloin's residence, Round Lake, near San Patricio

Texas. John McMullen signed the petition for San Antonio.[5] He was active in public life there and served as alderman in the years 1840 through 1844. In 1844 he sold most of his San Patricio property to McGloin.

John McMullen came to a tragic end. On January 21, 1853, he was brutally murdered, in what may have been a robbery attempt, in the two-story house he had built on the Market Street site where the old library building housing the Hertzberg Collection now stands. Strange tales are told of the "McMullen ghost." One story has it that James McGloin, in San Patricio, was talking to some friends when his father-in-law, John McMullen, appeared. All present saw him. He did not utter a sound but, with hands to his throat, seemed to be appealing to McGloin. After a few moments, the apparition disappeared. McGloin, convinced that something was wrong, saddled his horse and headed for San Antonio, a hard two-day ride. When he arrived the sheriff told him that his father-in-law had been murdered two days before. A current story holds that the ghost of John McMullen "walks" the building now on the site of his old home. The empresario has reputedly been seen on the staircases of the modern building—and it is said that he will continue to appear until the identity of his murderer is brought to light.

Texans would never have heard of James McGloin were it not for a missed embarkation. McGloin, born in County Sligo, Ireland, in 1799, had planned to emigrate to Australia but, at Liverpool, had missed the boat. That vessel was lost at sea, and, for some time, his family considered him dead. McGloin, however, had changed his mind about Australia and took ship for the New World, where he went to work for John McMullen in Mexico. Eventually, he became the older man's partner in the merchandising business at Matamoros and married Elizabeth Cummings, the daughter of McMullen's wife by her first marriage. They had six children. His wife died sometime prior to 1853, and he married Mary Murphy of County Kerry, Ireland.

For more than 25 years, McGloin devoted himself to the development and welfare of the San Patricio Colony. When, as a result of the Irish Potato Famine of 1846-1848, new waves of immigrants found their way to Texas, McGloin helped them get a start as settlers. He died June 19, 1856, and is buried in the old San Patricio Cemetery.[6]

The San Patricio Colony

The sailing ships of the early 1800's were designed primarily for cargo. Passengers were incidental and limited to the wealthy traveler for whom there might be a spare cabin. The days of mass emigration did not start until much later. Ships such as those hired by the Irish empresarios to convey the colonists from Ireland to New Orleans and from New York to Copano Bay had none of the conveniences or accommodations of later passenger service. The colonists occupied the area used for freight—the large unpartitioned hold.

Passengers brought their own bedding, and each family was assigned space for sleeping and cooking. The only privacy was that afforded by a sheet or curtain slung between sleeping areas. Since the vessel might be becalmed, fresh water was strictly rationed. Washing had to be done in seawater, which left an irritating cake of salt on skin and clothing. Consequently, there was little personal bathing on such a trip, which, in the case of a transatlantic voyage, might be a month or more. Sanitation facilities consisted of slop jars that were emptied over the side.

On occasion, the ship voyaged idyllically under clear skies with a fair wind and billowing sails through a silver-flecked sea. At such times the passengers could escape the crowded conditions of the hold to bask on deck in the invigorating breeze and clear sunshine. However, when storms threatened, all passengers had to go below; lights belowdecks were forbidden; the hatches were battened down; and sailors swarmed up the shrouds to reef sail far above the pitching deck.

Those in the hold, generally landlubbers all, huddled terrified in the darkness. Not knowing what was happening topside, their anxiety would be heightened with every pitch and roll of the vessel. At such times the seasickness of those not yet used to ocean travel added to the distress. The howling of the wind, answered by the protesting creaks of wave-battered timbers, must have sounded like an Irish banshee's *caoine* (dirge) announcing a grave in the deep.

Arriving at their destination was a joyous occasion, even though many who embarked in the bloom of health were by then physically weakened by the rigors of the trip. This lowered physical resistance may help explain the high mortality rate from disease of the Irish immigrants of the 1830's.

In October 1829 startling news reached the Mexican officials at La Bahía (Goliad). A band of Irish settlers from New York, recruited by McMullen and McGloin, had landed from the *Albion* at Matagorda and from the *New Packet* at Copano Bay. They were, according to the breathless messenger, in bad shape. No means of transportation had met them to conduct them and their supplies and implements to the interior. A vicious "norther," Texas's icy winter wind, was blowing, whipping the waters of the bay into whitecaps, and the colonists were huddled on the beach around small bonfires of driftwood.

Prospects looked bleak to those marrow-chilled immigrants on that wind-lashed shore of a strange land. Father Henry Doyle, who had accompanied them from New York, did his best to raise their spirits as he moved from group to group with words of encouragement.

At Goliad Father Miguel Muro, Alcalde José Aldrete, and Customs Officer Bonifacio Galán organized aid for the bewildered newcomers. Temporary housing was found for them at the abandoned Refugio Mission, and nearby Mexican ranchers provided warm food and clothing.[1]

A second group arrived on the *Albion* in December 1829, and a third in March 1830. All but a few who stayed at Copano were housed at Refugio. Toward the end of 1830, all the Irish families went westward to the Nueces River, where their lands were to be assigned to them. About 12 men remained in the vicinity of Refugio to harvest the crops which the immigrants had planted there.

On leaving Refugio Mission, the colonists had congregated near the Santa Margarita Crossing on the Nueces River, awaiting official confirmation of title to the lands they had selected. Mexican officialdom moved slowly, but, finally, the government appointed José Antonio Saucedo to allot the lands and issue titles. William O'Docharty, one of the colonists, was named surveyor.

On the American frontier, a town often simply grew up around a trading post, trail juncture, or small settlement. On the Spanish and, later, Mexican frontier, a town was often planned for a particular site on vacant lands, usually near a presidio, and town lots were sold to settlers of the area. They could elect an *ayuntamiento*, or town council.

> Among the families that arrived at the future Bee County area in October 1829 were those of Jeremiah O'Toole, James Brown, Patrick Hayes, James O'Connor, Patrick O'Boyle, William Quinn, and widow Mary Hart. These are noted as the original settlers of present-day Bee County.[2] Other settlers were the John Corrigan family near Aransas Creek; Pat Fadden, John Sweeney, David Kerr, Pat Carroll, and Charles Carter families on Poesta Creek; Pat Quinn, Timothy and Luke Hart, S.D. Callaghan, David Craven, and L. Carlisle on Papalote Creek; and H.T. Clare, Henry Ryan, and Eliza Clare near what is now Clareville.[3]

Four leagues square, beginning on the east bank of the Nueces River, were surveyed as the townsite of San Patricio de Hibernia (St. Patrick of Ireland). Streets, 20 *varas*, or 55 feet, wide, divided blocks that were 120 *varas*, or 330 feet, on each side. The central block or square was known as Constitutional Square. All streets ran north, south, east, and west from the borders of this square. The block fronting Constitutional Square on the east was reserved for a church and priests' dwelling; that on the west, for municipal buildings; and a block each for a market, jail, school, and burial ground.[4]

Thus, on October 24, 1831, San Patricio de Hibernia came into being. Among those who were confirmed in their grants at this time were James, Edward, John, and Patrick McGloin; John McMullen; John McSheany; John Heffernan; and George O'Docharty.[5]

In 1833 the schooner *Messenger* brought more colonists for the San Patricio Colony, but the captain refused to enter Aransas Pass because of bad weather and returned to New Orleans. Of those aboard, indications are that only the families of Thomas Pugh and Mark Killely came to Texas overland from New Orleans.[6] On May 16, 1834, the *Messenger* made port at Copano Bay with additional colonists. Aboard was Pat Carroll, whose wife had died of cholera and been buried at sea. Two other colonists had lost their husbands from the same cause—Mrs. Ann Burke and Mrs. Mary Carroll.[7] Within an hour after landing, and sheltered on the sun-baked beach at Copano by a sheet raised on posts, Mrs. Burke gave birth to a son, Patrick Burke, who later lived at Beeville. The infant was wet-nursed by an Indian woman from one of the local tribes.[8]

The Burkes, Carrolls, James Heffernans, and Simon Dwyer families traveled by oxcart to the confluence of Aransas and Poesta creeks. Here they found a small settlement of earlier arrivals, County Mayo and County Tipperary people. The settlement comprised the nephews and nieces of the Reverend John T. Molloy (who had succeeded Father Doyle) and the families of George O'Docharty and John Ryan.[9]

Among the San Patricio colonists, there was much dissatisfaction with the Mexican government. To them it seemed that the unhurried pace of Mexican

Margaret Heffernan Borland, daughter of John Heffernan, was a child among the first group of McMullen-McGloin colonists that arrived in Texas in 1829. Thrice widowed, she became a rancher in Victoria County. In 1873 she led a drive of her own cattle up the trail to Kansas, but died of "Trail Fever" shortly after she reached her destination.

administrative procedure added to the delays occasioned by the political turmoil within Mexico during the early 1830's. Many of the settlers (some of whom had occupied and cultivated their lands since 1829) were not confirmed in their titles until 1835. A number of settlers, in disgust, joined the Power-Hewetson Colony where there was no delay in the issuance of titles. Among these were Robert and James Carlisle; Bridget Quirk; Mary, Felix, Pat, and Timothy Hart; Daniel O'Boyle; Martin, Michael, and John O'Toole; and Patrick and William Quinn. [10]

The historic town of San Patricio is today almost abandoned. Shrubbery overgrows the site that, in 1836, housed a population of 500. At one time the thriving community was the county seat. Then, one catastrophe after another brought about its decline. In 1886 the railroad bypassed San Patricio and came to nearby Sinton. In 1889 the courthouse burned down, and many early records were lost. The county seat was then moved to Sinton. In 1893 the San Patricio St. Joseph's School and Convent were torn down to build the first Catholic Church in Sinton. The final blow to the struggling community was the damage of the hurricane of 1919, which devastated the area, destroying historic houses and the old St. Patrick's Church, the second built on the site, that had served the community since 1859.

St. Joseph's Convent and School (1876-1884), San Patricio

James McKeown's residence, San Patricio, 1979. Built in the late 1860's for Patrick Garaghty, the house is typical of the first frame dwellings built by the Irish settlers. There are no remaining examples of the earlier picket houses.

The Refugio Colony

The year was 1833. Four years before, the English Parliament had passed the Catholic Emancipation Act, which, after some 135 years, raised most of the disabilities that had been legislated against the Catholic Irish. However, the new legal provisions found little reflection in the practicalities of daily life. Irish tenants were still at the mercy of landlords, English mercantilist policy still bled Ireland economically, and the Catholic and Presbyterian Irish were still required by the tithing laws to give financial support to a church to which they did not belong.[1]

In the town of Ballygarrett in County Wexford, a ray of hope as bright as Texas sunshine appeared in the person of James Power. The Mexican empresario had returned to his homeland after an absence of 24 years to recruit settlers for Texas.

Notices and handbills in surrounding villages and counties had announced the purpose of his visit. Interested Irish crowded into the O'Brien cottage, home of Power's sister, Elizabeth, wife of Thomas O'Brien. Wide-eyed, they listened to Power's description of grassy plains and rich farmlands, of thousands of acres to be had almost for the asking, and of a way of life free from the restrictions of their present condition. Many must have shaken their heads in disbelief, but many did believe his report.

More than 250 families elected to accompany the empresario to Texas.[2] Little did they know that, like Moses of old, some would glimpse the promised land but never enter. Their bones would lie in Louisiana, in Copano Bay, and in the

Marker commemorating the Irish colonists, Rufugio, 1995. Surrounding the base are pavers inscribed with names of colonists, descendants of colonial settlers, and later residents of the area.

sands of St. Joseph and Mustang islands. One account states that of the 108 persons who left on the first ship for the New World, only eight reached the Texas colony.[3]

In December of 1833, the emigrants traveled from their homes in Ireland to Liverpool, England, where they were to board ship for Texas. Each family had provided itself with farming implements, seed, and enough provisions for one year. They paid Power about $30 per adult for transportation to Copano, Texas. After an abortive start, the first group finally left on January 8, 1834, on the ship *Prudence* and disembarked at New Orleans to await the others. The *Prudence* brought a second group, which disembarked at the Louisiana port on April 21, 1834. Each crossing took about four weeks.

Meanwhile, with several hundred more colonists, Power had left Liverpool on a larger ship, *The Heroine*, on March 12, 1834. Bad weather drove *The Heroine* off course, and it arrived in New Orleans two and a half months after leaving Liverpool.[4] Bad news awaited Power at New Orleans. An epidemic of cholera was sweeping the United States at the time, and the colonists waiting at the Gulf port had been stricken. Some had already died, and others were confined to the hospital.

Eager to leave the pest-ridden city, those of the immigrants who were apparently healthy boarded two schooners, *Sea Lion* and *Wildcat*, for the last leg of the trip. A furious gale was blowing as the vessels approached Aransas Pass. Both ships got over the bar at the pass entrance, but the *Wildcat* was thrown (or steered) into the shallows, and the *Sea Lion* ended up stuck in a mudbank. Although no lives were lost at this time, many of the supplies and implements were.

After the vessels grounded and before the passengers could be taken off, cholera, contracted in New Orleans, broke out again. The Mexican authorities would not allow the colonists to land until the epidemic had abated. The disease took a heavy toll. One colonist reports that, while aboard the ships, about 250 died and were buried in the waters of the bay. Some were taken by small boat and buried on St. Joseph's Island. Great must have been the despair and desolation of the survivors seeing their loved ones dying without the religious rites that were such a comforting part of their lives and then consigning the bodies to a watery grave so far from their homeland.

When the colonists were allowed to land, they had to spend another period in quarantine at Copano. Power, in his letter and plea of May 23, 1834, for help to Ramon Musquiz at San Antonio, noted that "they are enduring a great deal of hardship because the captains abandoned two endangered ships, losing most of the household goods, farming implements, tools, looms, and forges. . . ." He also noted that he had ". . . left some 70 people in the hospitals of New Orleans who are to come as soon as they improve. . . ."[5] It is estimated that one-third of all those who left Ireland had perished and that the adult Celtic manpower was reduced by one-half.[6]

Musquiz, the political chief of San Antonio, and Power's father-in-law, Don Felipe, came to the colonists' aid. They made arrangements for the transport of the survivors to Refugio and provided them with housing and supplies.

The Mexican government appointed José Vidaurri y Borrego on June 19, 1834, as commissioner to oversee the surveys and to grant titles to the colonists. In July of 1834, he set up the *ayuntamiento* (town council) of Refugio. The first *alcalde* (mayor) was John Dunn. Council members were Joshua Davis; James Brown; and James, John, and Martin Power. A local company of militia was formed with James Power as lieutenant colonel.[7]

James Bray was named surveyor to lay out the town of Refugio. He was assisted by Michael Fox, John Kelly, and Timothy Hart. The sale of town lots was held on August 4; that day lots were purchased by James Brown, Nicholas Fagan, Robert Patrick Hearne, Edward McDonough, John Malone, John Dunn, Samuel Blair, Joshua Davis, and James Bray.[8]

Titles to land within the colony were also distributed in August 1834, and among the first grantees were Isabella (Elizabeth) O'Brien, William Burke, and John Sinnott. At this time Joshua Davis, as a native of Ireland but a long-time

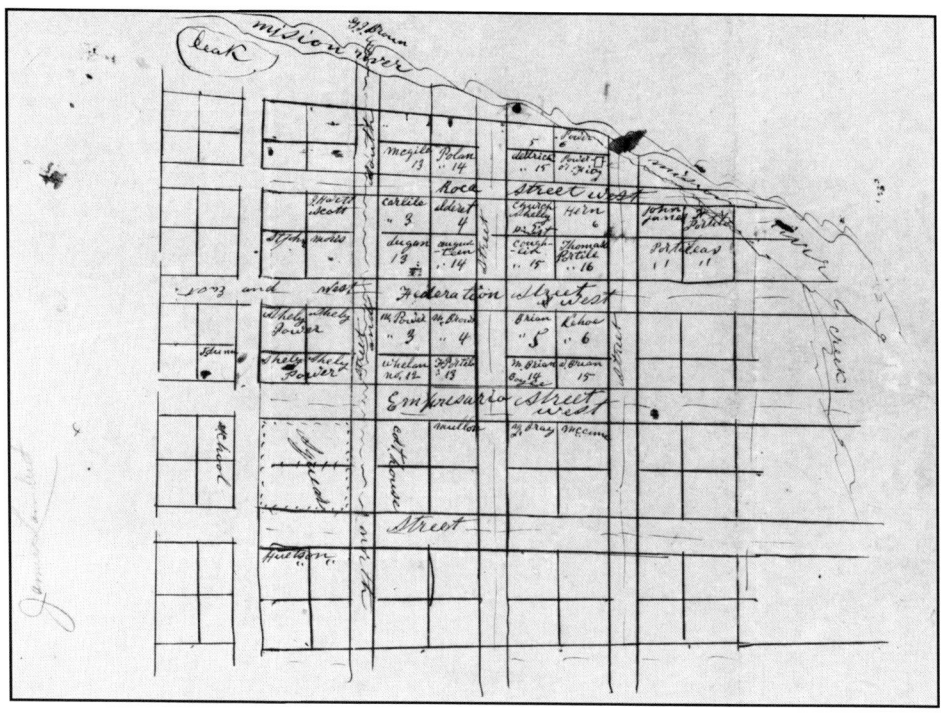

Plan drawing of Refugio by colonist Walter Lambert. The original plat of the town, with streets emanating from the principal square (lower left), followed the plan specified by the laws of the Mexican state of Coahuila y Texas.

resident of Texas, was confirmed in his title to land previously purchased on the San Antonio River. Within the five-month period, August through December, almost 220 leagues of land had been deeded to 201 grantees.[9]

The Refugio Colony, like that at San Patricio, was not all Irish. The empresarios of both colonies were obliged to guarantee rights and property to the Mexican families already residing within the area. The Power-Hewetson contract also called for the settlement of 100 Mexican families in addition to the Irish. Also, a number of land seekers, who were neither Irish nor Mexican, came through Refugio. Power urged them to remain within the colony and procured a contract amendment authorizing the issuance of land titles to those individuals who were not originally eligible.

The composition of the original Irish in the Refugio Colony differed from that of those in the San Patricio Colony. Many of the Power Colony Irish came directly from the southeastern corner of Ireland for the purpose of colonization in Texas. Those who came to the San Patricio Colony were more representative of Ireland as a whole. Most of them had originally come to Philadelphia and

Our Lady of Refuge Church, Refugio. This church (1868-1900) was built with stone from the Spanish mission which once stood on the same site. The interior view shows statues of Irish saints Patrick and Bridget above each end of the main altar.

Residence of Mary Frances Power Woodworth, granddaughter of James Power, in Refugio, c. 1910. Later owners named it "Ballygarrett" after the village in County Wexford, Ireland, where Power recruited colonists.

New York and were recruited there by McMullen and McGloin. They differed not only in their accents but, among themselves, in outlook and tradition as well. Some say the San Patricio colonists were better mixers, more convivial, and more contentious than their fellow countrymen at Refugio. The latter were considered aloof, reserved, and even clannish.

Today in Refugio County, lands of the old Mexican grants are still in the hands of descendants of the original Power-Hewetson colonists. In some cases the ranches are smaller because they were divided among children or parts were sold off. Other holdings are larger because they grew through purchase or through land warrants—lands given by the Republic of Texas for service in the Texas Revolution.

Families have intermarried so that the many branches of today's McGuills, Fagans, Lamberts, Powers, O'Connors, O'Briens, Foxes, etc., are all related. As one Refugian put it—"Down here, you dassent say a bad word about any of us, 'cuz chances are you're talking to a relative."

Everyday Life in the Colonies

The colonists, in traveling to their lands, generally hauled their goods by oxcart. Where small groups of individual settlers were isolated, they often established "settlements." This did not mean villages on the European order, only that the homes were relatively close. Examples are the Poesta and Papalote Creek settlements of the San Patricio Colony and the Fagan settlement of the Refugio Colony. For the Irish, coming from a land of year-round moderate temperature, the extremes of Texas weather were particularly harsh and sometimes unexpected. One pioneer tells of traveling cross-country to his grant in lovely weather, going into camp under a beautiful starlit sky, and being wakened in the night by a furious, bone-chilling norther blowing across the plains.[1]

On arrival at their destination, the first concern was "making a crop," generally corn. The settlers also experimented with cabbage and other crops that had been familiar to them in Ireland. Initially, for mutual protection against Indians, crop plantings were on a communal basis. They worked together in the clearing of small plots, then planted and harvested together, dividing the proceeds.[2] In later times, for protection against marauding bandits, they went back to this system.

Sugar and coffee were obtained from Mexican traders by bartering. Food did not have much variety, but it was substantial and nutritious. Staples were bacon, jerked beef, coffee— and corn cakes, when the corn could be milled. Hand mills were at first used for grinding corn. Before grinding, the corn was thrown on hot embers to drive out the weevils, then husked in lye.[3] Flour was purchased through coastal import traders such as Power, who set up warehouses at places such as Copano.

Game was plentiful in Texas, and the meals included venison, wild turkey, and squirrel. Soon small vegetable gardens and fruit trees added to the fare. Water was supplied by wells or from nearby creeks. If the stream dried up, a shallow hole was dug in the streambed where there were a number of rocks, and spring water was usually found.[4] One pioneer noted that ". . . we drank water from creeks, barrels, ponds, and cow tracks," and they had few of the many diseases that afflict modern man.[5]

In rural Ireland, from which most of these settlers came, houses were built of collected fieldstone. The roofs were thatched with wheat straw bound down with willow saplings. The housing construction skills acquired in the homeland were of no value in early Texas, where rock had to be quarried and other materials were not available.

The first houses were made of upright poles standing side by side, the spaces between chinked with grass or moss. White sand from a creek bed was a common floor. Roofs were made of split boards or thatched with palmetto; chimneys were built with sticks and moss plastered on the inside with clay to make them fireproof. Later, cabin-style houses were built of logs with floors of smoothed boards.

A pioneer, Mrs. Annie Fagan Teal, tells of her father cutting the logs for the house with a whipsaw and flooring it with boards taken from a wrecked and abandoned Spanish ship.[6] Those who did not have such a handy source of planks could purchase boards from the commercial houses on the coast. Inland, where rocks could be dug from the hillsides, stone houses were built. When first dug out, the rocks were moist and easily cut. They were then left in the sun to dry and harden before being used in the walls. When the Indians were still a threat, the settlers often constructed a small brush pen or corral at the rear of the house, with no entrance except that provided by the rear door of the dwelling. When Indians were known to be in the neighborhood, the milk cows, oxen, and saddle horses were driven through the house into this pen.[7]

Herds of mustangs, descendants of strayed or lost Spanish horses, roamed the plains. These the settlers attempted to tame. They would first capture one, place a stuffed dummy of a man on his back, then set him loose. The horse would attempt to rejoin the herd, but the others, spooked by the "rider," would try to outrun him. "This would start every mustang for miles around to running," recounted one pioneer. The thunder of thousands of hoofs "sounded like the roar of a cyclone." After the herd had run itself down, the settlers would guide it between wide entrance arms of brush into a corral. The adult mustang was, tired or not, still difficult to tame.[8]

They had better success with the foals they caught and put to suckle with a cow. As the foals grew older, they were trained and used as the famous "Texas cow ponies." Transportation was primarily by horseback, and, before buggies or wagons could be built, drag sleds were used. These were flat beds built of tree limbs and moved on runners made of smoothed logs.[9] They were particularly useful in mud or over prairie grass.

Could the formidable Texas mosquito, coupled with ranch isolation, have been responsible for the loss in Texas of much of the Irish oral tradition?

Ireland enjoys a long twilight—a half-dark, half-light days-end period—without mosquitoes! Because of the proximity of neighbors, this was the time for visiting. Neighbors would, as they had for centuries, gather around the firesides; news would be exchanged and stories told; and Irish and European history, old Irish legends, and even the mythology of ancient Greece and Rome would be recounted—with surprising accuracy. The children would sit listening in silent wonder and absorb the rudiments of a classical education together with a reaffirmation of pride in the "Irish identity."

In the storytellers' skilled recounting of the ancient legends, young imaginations would people the flickering shadows of the fire-lit room with a procession of legendary heroes. Cuchullen would appear, single-handedly defending his king and province against Queen Maeve's invading army. Young listeners would share his anguish as duty requires him to fight and slay his dearest friend. When the mighty warrior is mortally wounded, they join in his final act of defiance as he binds himself to an upright stone so that, in death, he may face his enemies on his feet. At another time the deep shadows would give way to the splendor of the beautiful palaces and sunlit land of Tir na nOg (The Land of Youth) far over the western sea. To this land of the ever-young, Ossian, son of the great Finn Macool, was transported by his faerie bride. He left it to visit his native land, but, when he involved himself in the concerns of the men of Ireland, he became an aging mortal and could never return to the enchanted land.

In early Texas there were no regular fireside gatherings. There were no close neighbors, outside of towns. The workday was from sunup to sundown, and the fast-gathering darkness marked bedtime. With windows and doors open to take advantage of the cool of evening, lights were discouraged because of the clouds of mosquitoes and other insects they attracted. Screens did not come into general use until the beginning of the 20th century, and the only defense against the winged bloodsuckers was the rather ineffective and nearly as annoying smudge pot.[10]

The children of the family had the chores usual to those living on a farm or ranch. The girls learned to cook, launder, sew, embroider, and look after the house; and the boys helped in farming, caring for the livestock, and hunting and trapping wild animals. While still in their teens, most children had to assume adult responsibilities.

One of the youngest soldiers of the Texas Revolution was 13-year-old Thomas John O'Brien.[11] Henry Scott, 10 years old, was part of an Indian-hunting party

Cistern built to store rainwater on the prairie, O'Brien homestead near the Fagan Settlement, Refugio County

Gathering after Sunday Mass, Gussettville, c. 1910. Parishioners from the surrounding ranches often visited in the shade near the Nueces River before returning home.

when captured by Lipans.[12] James Hart, 11 years old, was captured by Indians while rounding up livestock.[13] One of the wagon drovers hauling supplies from Corpus Christi to Fort Merrill was 16-year-old Patrick Burke.[14] The father and uncles of Merle Kelly of Refugio were driving wagons at 13 and "out on their own" at 15.[15]

A father in those days was as concerned as any today in his daughter's choice of a husband. Nicholas Fagan was no exception. He had some misgivings about the 19-year-old Irish lad who called on his daughter Mary. The hardworking Fagan had planted crops, raised cattle on his land, and had built a spacious two-story house for his family. By comparison, his daughter's suitor, who "batched" with another young man, spent much of his time hunting when not serving with the Texas army.

In his musings on the situation, Fagan was aware that the youngster had acquired a Mexican grant of 4,400 acres and that, for service with the Texas army, he had added to that acreage. But what was he going to do with all that land? Oh, he could work when he had a mind to! A Mexican craftsman had taught him how to make saddletrees, and, with the proceeds from these, he had purchased his first horse. One thing at least was in his favor: he did not come to pay formal court to Mary Fagan without first outfitting himself in new apparel. That had meant more saddletrees! "Still," mused Nicholas Fagan, "I'm afraid he won't amount to much."[16]

Reluctantly he consented to Mary's marriage to Thomas O'Connor, and part of her dowry included some cattle from the Fagan herds. Those cattle formed the nucleus of the vast herds that made Thomas O'Connor one of the largest cattle ranchers in the state as well as one of its biggest landowners.

Wresting a living from the land under trying circumstances did not leave much time for social life. However, when the colonists did come together, whether for a wedding or a wake, such occasions were savored as a time of joyous reunion of families and friends. A wedding was a time to celebrate, and, following the ceremonies honoring the bride and groom, the young folks danced into the night, and the elders swapped Texas tales or exchanged news of the old country. After Texas joined the Union, the Fourth of July was a day-long celebration in some of the small settlements. Families came in from the surrounding ranches to celebrate Independence Day. One such celebration at Refugio was described by old-timer E.R. "Scrub" Kelly as ". . . a tournament in the morning . . . a big free barbecue at noon . . . the afternoon devoted to horse racing, and a big dance at night."

The tournament was a competition in which horsemen vied with each other in spearing rings from eight posts spaced at 40-foot intervals. Each rider carried a six- to eight-foot pike sharpened at the end and, with this under his arm, rode full tilt for the rings. "He was scored on the number of rings speared and the elapsed time on the course."[17]

John E. Moody, nephew of John J. Linn, wearing tournament costume, Victoria, early 1870's

Tournament knight, Refugio, c. 1905

The Texas of pioneer days was not as shrub-covered as today's acres of mesquite would indicate. Old-timers tell of seas of waving prairie grass in areas now covered by mesquite and pin oak. Occasional prairie fires would sweep across the plains, destroying the tall grass and also the slow-growing mesquite shoots. The roads and wagon trails that came with intercommunity trading became barriers that limited the spread of grass fires. Birds and cattle did the rest. Mexican wagon drovers who fed their mules on mesquite beans also accounted for the proliferation of the mesquite tree.[18]

The pioneers who had extensive lands turned to ranching and stock raising. This is still the occupation of the families living some distance from the coast. The Foxes, Fagans, O'Briens, and O'Connors are just a few of the families that still engage in stock raising. Toward the end of the last century, those who held lands closer to the coast turned from stock raising to farming. The rich loam of that area made it ideal for crops.

In early Texas those who lived on isolated ranches were often spared the ravages of cholera, smallpox, and yellow fever that devastated the more populous areas. However, that very isolation made them vulnerable to another scourge—marauding whites and raiding Indians. Of the Indians, the Comanches were the worst. Theirs was one of the few Indian tribes that moved at night. Isolated Texas settlers dreaded the bright moonlit nights of spring, summer, and autumn that became known as "the Comanche moon." On such nights, when all nature seemed to peacefully sleep beneath the glow of a golden moon, the silence was apt to be shattered by the cries of attacking Comanches.

Wild animals occasionally caused concern, as indicated by the following incident recounted by Mrs. Hallie Fagan Snider: "The John Fagans made their home at what is known as 'The Placeto.' One day while Mr. Fagan was working cattle and Mrs. Fagan was alone, she parked their small son Peter in a box and set him out in the yard under a tree. Soon after returning to the house, Mrs. Fagan looked out a window to see how the baby was doing and saw a wolf trotting around the baby's box. She rushed out and chased the wolf away."

The small ranch graveyards bear mute testimony to the harsh life. Infant mortality was high, and few family plots are without infants' graves.

Since most of the Irish settlers were Catholic, provision was always made for a chapel in which Mass could be celebrated when a visiting priest came by. When Nicholas Fagan built his ranch house, he reserved the upper story as a chapel—complete with altar, confessional, and priest's room.[19] His own Catholicism and that of the vaqueros prompted Dennis O'Connor, grandson of Nicholas Fagan, to erect a chapel on his ranch. The religious practices of the Old Country were often retained and handed down to the descendants. Present-day residents of the Irish colonies tell of the practice of the nightly family rosary continued into their lifetimes and of the "Black Fast." The Black Fast as observed in Ireland was a far more rigorous abstention from food during Lent than

St. Anthony's Chapel (1900-1942), O'Connor Ranch on the San Antonio River, Refugio County, 1933. After it was destroyed by a hurricane, the O'Connor family built St. Dennis Chapel, a masonry structure patterned after Mission Espada.

that specified by the Church. Those who engaged in manual labor were exempt from fasting. However, many of the early settlers did not avail themselves of this exemption. Joseph Fagan, a blacksmith, was one who observed the fast. His family records that, on at least one occasion during the Black Fast, he was so weak from fasting that he tottered as he walked.[20] The consecration of the family to the Sacred Heart of Jesus is today, as it has been for generations, a strong devotion in Ireland. Shrines similar to those used in Ireland are still seen in the South Texas homes of Irish descendants.

Those who settled near the coast or at points that were trail crossings or wagon trail terminals did so because of employment opportunities or trading possibilities. Since little money was in circulation, work was exchanged for clothing, farm animals, or farm produce. These were traded for other needed

Oscar G. Fagan in front of Peter H. Fagan's ranch house, Refugio County, c. 1898. Located near the site of the original Fagan homestead, the house was built in 1868 by Irish-born Michael O'Keefe, a carpenter in Victoria.

The Book of Brands *in the Refugio County Courthouse contains cattle brands and ear markings registered by Irish colonists.*

items. Some gristmills were eventually set up, but most flour was imported from New Orleans, as were "bacon hams," blankets and dry goods, coffee, sugar, building lumber and hardware, whiskey, tobacco, and wagon frames. Continuing the trade begun in Spanish times, mules and horses purchased from Mexican traders were auctioned off in Louisiana and trade goods purchased with the proceeds.[21] Even though, for the time, the annual license fee for "vending goods, wares, and merchandise" was high—$100—profits were also high. Some coastal traders made small fortunes.

An 1857 bill of lading listing goods shipped from New Orleans to Refugio County via Powder Horn (Indianola)

Two Would-be Towns and a Texas Frontier Storekeeper

In early Texas the ranchers, with their extensive herds, and the import-export traders, with their bulging warehouses, were few compared to the number of laborers, professional men, and small merchants who provided the developing economy with the services and small capital investments that gave it stability and strength.

In some instances the site of a lonely frontier trading post marked the beginning of a later-flourishing town like Corpus Christi. In others, the trader provided the necessary goods and services; his store became a business terminal and social center—the only link between a wild, untamed frontier and civilization. Then, as other centers developed and the land filled up, the small community died aborning, leaving only a place-name. Such was the fate of Blanconia, Gussettville, Indianola, and others.

The town of Gussettville was founded in the 1850's when a North Carolina veteran of the Mexican War, Norwick Gussett, established a trading post near the Nueces River and southeast of the present town of George West. The site was a coach stop on the San Antonio-Corpus Christi route. Gussett eventually opened a general store there "carrying everything from coffins to groceries." Gussettville was in the San Patricio land grant area and served the surrounding ranchers—many of whom were Irish born. Its most prosperous period was the 1860's. The town was abandoned when the railroad bypassed it, and today all that remains is the wooden St. Joseph's Catholic Church located in a cemetery

St. Joseph's Church, Gussettville, c. 1910

that bears mute testimony to the Irish who peopled the area. Tombstones, bearing dates of death from 1835, record settlers from the Irish counties of Leitrim, Roscommon, Sligo, and Fermanagh, as well as from "Ireland" generally. On many tombstones the word "Leitrim" is spelled phonetically as the Irish would pronounce it—"Lathrem."

Blanconia was similar to Gussettville and suffered a similar fate.[1] Irish-born William McGuill had fought at San Jacinto and afterwards retired to his land grant on Blanco Creek. When he died he left his property to his nephew, Thomas, and other heirs in Ireland. Thomas came to Texas in 1853 to claim the land and later bought out the other heirs. In order to bring his wife and family to Texas, he became a peddler. He bought goods at Old St. Mary's near Copano, transported the wares by packhorse, and sold them at isolated ranches. At the

Thomas and Mary McGuill

same time, he took orders for future delivery. In 1857 he brought his wife, Mary O'Reilly McGuill, and their two children to a log cabin on Dog Branch Creek. Their third child, Martin, was born here in 1858. Of their 10 children, two died as infants and are buried at Dog Branch. Arrangements were made with the mission at Refugio, some 15 miles away, for a priest to visit once a month to conduct religious services at the McGuill home.

  Meanwhile, Thomas McGuill was building a more spacious house and a store on his land on Blanco Creek. He set aside an acre of ground on which he built a log church in 1875. He furnished it himself and donated the church and site to the Catholic Diocese. In 1890 he built a larger church to replace the first building. The log church and the later one were on the east side of the Blanco and were both known as our Lady of the Rosary. The second building served until

1926, when it was torn down and replaced, on the west side of the Blanco, with the present St. Catherine's Church. The statue of Our Lady of the Rosary and the Stations of the Cross from the old church are in St. Catherine's.

With the outbreak of the Civil War, Thomas became a tailor for the Confederacy, leaving the running of the store to his wife and family. Times were hard. Merchandise was almost unobtainable because of the Federal blockade of Texas ports. Some goods were obtained through the courage and ingenuity of a woman named Sally Scull. She owned some land near that of the McGuills and, with a band of Mexican drovers, smuggled cotton into Mexico, bringing back ammunition for the Confederacy and supplies for her neighbors.[2] Sally Scull dressed like a man, wore two pistols, was a dead shot with either pistol or rifle, liked a Mexican fandango, and was an astute poker player. She was also described as a "merciless killer when aroused" and "possessor of a vocabulary that would put a trooper to shame."[3]

With Thomas away, life in the prairie store was lonely for Mrs. McGuill. The days would be busy enough operating a store and keeping track of a number of small, active children. However, at night, with the children asleep and the mournful howl of the coyote the only sound, the silent menace of the darkened prairie caused anxious moments. On Thomas's return after the war, conditions improved for the store, and, with the help of his son Martin, he could now concentrate on farming and stock raising. He made Martin a partner in the store in the early 1870's.

In June of 1874, an incident occurred that resulted in Thomas McGuill becoming a banker of sorts for the community. Refugio County rancher Thad Swift had sold a load of wool and deposited the proceeds for safekeeping in Refugio, but someone thought that he had taken the money home with him. Thieves broke into the Swift home, dragged the man and his wife into the yard, where they murdered them, and ransacked the house for the money. Other settlers in the area did not want to keep sums of money at their isolated ranches and resolved, after the Swift murders, to let it be known that money was not kept on their premises. Thomas McGuill bought a safe, and the other settlers, trusting him as a friend and businessman, deposited their money with him at the store.

In the 1880's the McGuills moved their store to the west bank of the Blanco and added a cotton gin, gristmill, and blacksmith shop. The first telephone line, put through from Beeville in 1889, ended at the McGuill store. Martin was a partner in the company and was made manager. He later bought out his associates and, when the lines were extended to Refugio, sold the company to Southwestern Bell. He also served as postmaster for the little community now called Blanconia.

Life in Blanconia was a busy one for Martin McGuill as postmaster, banker, cotton ginner, meat and corn grinder, blacksmith, telephone manager, and

A Sunday gathering at the McGuill home, Blanconia

The McGuill store, Blanconia, c. 1904

storekeeper. The daily routine was lightened by the shopping trips of the settlers and the exchange of news and gossip. Occasionally, an unusual event would add to the local news. One morning Martin opened the sugar barrel to fill a customer's order, but the barrel was empty. At the bottom was a neatly drilled hole, through which he could see the ground some three feet below the store flooring. Sugar had been strewn about on the outside, and the trail ended where it had apparently been loaded into a buggy. The thief obviously worked at night with an exact knowledge of where to drill. How he had done so was a topic of much discussion.

Changes were coming to the frontier communities, and sometimes these were incomprehensible to the older folks. Old-time Blanconia resident "Buck" Emmert tells of his grandfather who, though familiar with the steam engine, was unable to understand the mysteries of the internal-combustion automobile. He would never ride in one without first checking the "boiler" (radiator) and was baffled no end by the ability of the machine to move without first "building up a head of steam."

Until 1950 three generations of McGuills were local merchants. In that year the third McGuill store building was torn down. Blanconia, halfway between Refugio and Beeville, had served its purpose. The railroad had come to other towns and bypassed the little trading center. The area is still known as Blanconia, but all that remains of the McGuill settlement is St. Catherine's Church and, across the creek, the cemetery. The half-acre graveyard is surrounded by a fence to protect it from the cattle that graze nearby and the deer that browse on surrounding shrubbery. Thomas McGuill had donated this land, and he was the first to be buried there; his grave and that of his wife are surrounded by graves of the many later McGuills and in-laws.[4]

Pro-Mexican Irish?

Questions have been raised about the Irish colonists' support of the Texas cause in the revolt against Mexico. Some Irish, like some of their Anglo-Saxon neighbors, supported Mexico, but the Irish colonists in general wholeheartedly supported the revolutionary cause. In fact, they had demanded independence at a time when it was unpopular among other Texans.

Texans were far from unanimous in the first and second phases of their revolt. The first phase did not claim independence but, rather, was the assertion of rights under the Mexican Constitution of 1824. Leaders were at first split between a War Party, believing in armed assertion, and a Peace Party, believing in conciliation.[1] In the second phase, including a declaration and war for independence, there were yet many who, content with the prosperity they enjoyed under Mexico, did not support armed resistance.

For purposes of political administration, the Mexican province of Texas was divided into the three departments of Nacogdoches, Brazos, and Béxar. The Irish colonies were part of Béxar. The DeWitt, Austin, and other colonies farther east were in the other two departments. Texas itself was part of the combined state of Coahuila y Tejas.

In the 1830's Santa Anna came to power in Mexico as a supporter of Federalism—Mexican "states rights." Once in power, however, he switched to Centralism and ordered the disarming of the states and the disbanding of militia units. The Mexican states rose in revolt, and Governor Agustín Viesca of Coahuila y

Tejas called on all Texans for armed aid to resist Centralism. The militias of San Antonio and Victoria responded. He received no aid from the colonies east of the Guadalupe River nor from the Irish colonies.[2] Santa Anna brutally suppressed the armed opposition in the southern Mexican states. In the state of Zacatecas, 2,000 citizens opposing Centralism were killed. Texans knew what was coming. In June of 1835, Texas citizens meeting at San Felipe in the Austin colony, in a courageous action, issued a strong declaration defending the federal and state constitutions. Conservative groups there opposed the strong language of the declaration. A group at Gonzales, at a meeting on July 7, went so far as to pledge loyalty to the nation, citing as evidence their refusal to supply Governor Viesca with militiamen.[3]

Santa Anna was not impressed by pledges of loyalty. He dispatched General Martín Perfecto de Cos to disarm Texas. During this period a Declaration of Independence was drawn up at Goliad and signed by 91 citizen-soldiers, including 42 from the Irish colonies. When presented to the provisional Texas government at San Felipe, it was repudiated and suppressed. Texas independence was not declared until March 2, 1836, two and a half months later at Washington-on-the-Brazos.

An armed confrontation in January 1836 attests to the sharp division among Texans on "constitutional rights under Mexico" and "independence for Texas." It was the Texas Irish—some of whom were later accused of supporting Mexico— who were among those supporting independence.

Some Texans had banded together and successfully attacked San Antonio, held by Cos. Following the capture of San Antonio, a group of men under Colonel James Grant started for Matamoros to link up with Mexican Federalists. Hoping to obtain supplies at Goliad, they marched by way of Presidio La Bahía, which was occupied by Captain Phillip Dimmitt and his garrison. Seeing the Goliad Flag of Independence flying from the walls of the presidio, Grant ordered it taken down, stating they were Federalists and would stand by the Mexican Constitution of 1824. Dimmitt disagreed, arguing that Grant and his men were acting against Texan interests. At first he refused to furnish them with supplies. Times were indeed confused. The men on each side were drawn up in battle-ready lines, but the matter was finally settled without bloodshed.[4]

There were many Texans, including Irish, who at first hesitated to take up arms against Mexico. If nothing else, their economic interests prompted hesitancy. Later reminiscences of old settlers hark back to those days prior to the revolution as ones of "peace and plenty."[5]

Additional considerations influenced the Irish—particularly those of San Patricio. Their descendants say today that many felt a loyalty to a government that had given them land and freedom and economic opportunity. They had come first to the northeastern United States in the 1820's and 1830's and found themselves the targets of a violent anti-Irish "nativism." Their coming to Texas was

Detail of duty report from Captain Phillip Dimmitt's garrison, Goliad, December 21, 1835. Among those present were Morgan O'Brien, James Burke, John Dunn, Timothy Hart, Michael O'Donnell, and other Irish colonists.

largely because of the denial of economic opportunity and social acceptance in the United States. In Mexico, they found a hospitable Mexican community and economic freedom.

Coming to the Mexican province of Texas in 1829, they had had six years to get acquainted with Mexicans who showed them how to use the resources of this strange land to meet everyday needs. They had shown them the proper methods of cultivation for the climate and had introduced them to new feed crops, cattle, and vegetables.[6] Their close social and commercial contact with the Mexican settlers was bound to promote understanding of Hispanic values. They traded with the Mexicans south of the Nueces River, so the latter built a road in the early 1830's from Matamoros to San Patricio to facilitate that trade. Its completion was the occasion for a four-day fiesta in honor of the San Patricio Irish.[7] The town of Banquete is on the site of and named for this celebration.

Their brother Celts of Refugio, having come directly from Ireland, were happily spared the "northern experience" of the United States, but, arriving as late as 1834, they had little time in which to develop a rapport with the natives of their new country.

The San Patricio Irish would have shown themselves insensitive and ungrateful to their Mexican neighbors had they not hesitated to take up arms on the side of the revolution. However, with the outbreak of hostilities, they discovered that the solid values of their neighbors were not reflected in the tyrannical government of Santa Anna. They then threw themselves wholeheartedly behind the Texan cause and into the conflicts at the Alamo, Goliad, San Patricio, and San Jacinto.

Many later-arriving Americans would not permit them to forget that they had initially wavered in their support of the Texas revolt. Their ranches were raided time and again, and some of them were driven from the area. Later, during the Mexican-American War, the formation by the Mexican army of a "San Patricio Battalion"–although having no connection with the settlement on the Nueces--revived animosity toward them.

There *were* Irishmen in Mexican service, however. Captain Ira Westover's report of the taking of Lipantitlán in November 1835 indicates a total of 14 Irishmen from San Patricio in the Mexican command. Five were in the fort when it was taken. He added that some were there by compulsion and some by choice.[8] John J. Linn's account states that the men of San Patricio were pressed into service by Captain Nicholas Rodríguez, Mexican commander at Lipantitlán.[9] Whatever the situation, there was apparently no doubt of the San Patricians' position 10 days later because, on November 14, Captain Phillip Dimmitt at Goliad wrote Stephen F. Austin, then in command of the Texas Army, advising him that all the citizens at San Patricio had joined the Texas cause.[10]

As further evidence of their participation, there is the letter written on February 22, 1836, by James McGloin at San Patricio to Colonel James W. Fannin, then commanding at Goliad, outlining the situation in the Irish settlement. McGloin pointed out that, as regulars and volunteers, there were 100 San Patricians in the field, leaving only 16 men to protect the families then being threatened by hostile Indians.[11] McGloin himself refused to surrender a cannon to Mexican forces. Captain Rodríguez finally obtained it, but only after threatening to lash McGloin to it.

The much-quoted diary of Dr. Joseph Henry Barnard, one of those spared by the Mexicans at the Goliad Massacre, notes that the San Patricio families remained at that place and sought the protection of the Mexican army. The doctor was apparently ignorant of the fact that many of his fellow prisoners at Goliad, later executed, were in fact San Patricians.[12] Other sources indicate that, during the Goliad campaign, most of the San Patricio families had moved east to Victoria and that the town was burned.

Like the San Patricio Colony, Refugio included a number of Mexican settlers. Refugio came under suspicion of supporting Mexico because General Cos's army had been able to raise two military units there. These units were composed of Mexican colonists and were recruited by colonists Carlos de la Garza and Manuel Sabriego.[13]

This apparently split the settlement. The Irish colonists of Refugio were among the first Texans for independence. In the ensuing conflict, the town of Refugio was burned and colonists' homes and crops were destroyed and their cattle driven off. Within six months an estimated one-third of the manpower of this Irish colony lay in soldiers' graves.[14] The colonial area had turned into a bloody battlefield.

Some Irish families may have remained loyal to Mexico, but if any further evidence of the general commitment of the Irish colonies to the Texas cause is needed, the proceedings of the temporary government of Texas should be conclusive. Before adjournment on March 17, 1836, a resolution was introduced to the convention asking that agents and quartermasters be instructed to furnish rations and supplies to the San Patricio, Refugio, and San Antonio families because the husbands and fathers were in the field and the families had been driven by the enemy from their homes.[15]

The First Skirmishes

On September 20, 1835, James Power was at his Live Oak Point home on Copano Bay when he observed a Mexican ship entering the bay. In a small boat, he and another man followed the Mexican vessel to its landing site and discovered that this was the troopship of Mexican General Martín Perfecto de Cos and 500 men, sent by Santa Anna to disarm Texas. Walter Lambert was immediately dispatched to the other colonies with the news.[1] By the next night, while Cos's men were still unloading supplies, the colonies in the interior had news of the landing.

The Mexican general remained in the vicinity for about 10 days, and, during that time, he and his officers visited Power's home, giving rise to the story that they were "entertained" there. He then took up the march for San Antonio. At Refugio Captains Carlos de la Garza and Manuel Sabriego raised, from among the Mexican settlers of the Irish colony, two companies of rancheros for the Mexican army.

On the day the Mexicans reached Goliad, October 2, a historic confrontation occurred at Gonzales. Following Santa Anna's order to disarm the colonists, Captain Francisco Castañeda and 100 cavalrymen were sent from San Antonio to demand from the Gonzales settlers a cannon that had been given them for protection against the Indians. The settlers, under John H. Moore, refused with a defiant "Come and take it," emphasized by a blast of chain and scrap metal from the cannon. The settlers then advanced to the attack. Castañeda ordered a retreat to San Antonio, leaving one dead cavalryman on the field. Now Texas had its Lexington.

Leaving a garrison at Goliad, Cos advanced to San Antonio. He little realized that the men of the Irish colonies he had just left were moving to cut his supply route to Copano by capturing Goliad. John J. Linn of Victoria had sent word to Refugio of a planned expedition to capture Goliad and asked for help.[2] Ira Westover at Refugio sent messages to the surrounding ranchers with the call to arms. Eyewitness accounts vary as to specific details, but, in any case, on October 10 or 11, one or two contingents of volunteers, including quite a few Irishmen, arrived as reinforcements for the assaulting party.[3]

Soon after the capture of Goliad, John O'Toole and John Williams were dispatched to San Patricio to enlist the support of that colony. They were captured by the Mexicans and, in irons, compelled to work on the Lipantitlán fortifications. When word of this came back to Goliad, Westover led 35 men, including a number of Irish colonists, off to rescue the prisoners.[4] The group had grown somewhat by the time it reached Lipantitlán.

The main body of the garrison was absent from the fort, attempting to intercept Westover and his men, who had reached Lipantitlán undetected. James O'Reilly of San Patricio volunteered to go into the fort and persuade the 22 defenders to surrender.[5] Through his efforts the fort was captured without a shot on November 3. There the Texans discovered that the prisoners, O'Toole and Williams, had already been sent to Mexico. The citizen-soldiers left the fort on November 4, then, while recrossing the Nueces, were attacked by the return-ing garrison members.

In the ensuing 20-minute battle, the Mexicans suffered heavy losses before withdrawing into the fort. One Texan, William Bracken, was wounded. The Texans withdrew to the town of San Patricio and then to Goliad.[6]

Most of the Goliad garrison, including some Irish, went on to the Siege of Béxar (San Antonio) to drive Cos out. The Irish remaining at Goliad organized under Captain Phillip Dimmitt to hold Presidio La Bahía.

Goliad was important to the defense of San Antonio. Whoever held that frontier bastion controlled the supply route from the port at Copano to San Antonio. While the Texans held it, General Cos was unable to receive supplies or reinforcements. This capture of his supply route may have been a reason for

---

Irish in the Lipantitlán Battle, November 4, 1835

James Power; John Dunn; Nicholas and John Fagan; John, James, and Walter Lambert; Martin Lawlor; John, Michael, and Patrick Quinn; Charles Malone; Morgan and Thomas John O'Brien; James and Thomas O'Connor; Michael McDonough; James O'Reilly; Patrick and Michael O'Reilly; Daniel O'Driscoll; William Ryan; and Jeremiah O'Toole. [7]

Thomas John O'Brien, nephew of James Power, was 13 when he served in Dimmitt's garrison at Goliad. Bereft of his parents less than two years after they emigrated from Ireland, "John" followed his older brother, Morgan, and other Irish colonists who volunteered to secure Goliad from reoccupation by Mexican Centralist forces.

his surrender of San Antonio to a numerically smaller force.[8] After some bitter house-to-house fighting, Cos surrendered San Antonio on December 10, 1835. With the retirement of his forces beyond the Rio Grande, Texas enjoyed a brief respite. It was the calm before the storm.

The Consultation of Texas delegates at San Felipe in the Austin colony to the east had, on November 7, 1835, issued a declaration that Texans were fighting for their liberties as guaranteed by the Mexican Constitution of 1824. Independence—the second stage of the revolt—was not declared until March 2, 1836.

The men who had fought at Goliad, at Lipantitlán, and at the siege and taking of San Antonio had definite feelings about independence. On the 20th of December, 91 men under Captain Dimmitt signed what is known as the Goliad Declaration of Independence. There were 42 signers from the Irish colonies.[9]

On that same date, there was raised at Goliad one of the first flags of Texas independence. It was made by Dimmitt and depicted, against a white field, a red sinewy arm and hand grasping a red sword. In front of the assembled garrison, it was hoisted to the top of the flagstaff by Nicholas Fagan and Morgan O'Brien.[10] It is interesting to note that the design on the flag was similar to that which appears on the crests of many Irish families.

Depiction of Dimmitt's flag, painted in 1936 from a description in Nicholas Fagan's reminiscences

The Santa Anna Campaign

Convinced that he was the one to bring the Texans to heel, Santa Anna personally prepared a massive strike early in 1836. He sent General José Urrea to strike along the southern colonies while he marched to San Antonio.

Following the fall of San Antonio to revolutionary forces the previous December, the foreign volunteers there became restless, and a march was planned on Matamoros to join with Mexican Federalists. General Sam Houston, now commanding the Texas army, had advised against this division of forces. However, F.W. Johnson and Dr. James Grant left for San Patricio with 60 men and three cannons to make that town their headquarters for the Matamoros expedition. Fannin prepared Goliad for the expected Mexican invasion.

Urrea, informed of the presence of Grant and Johnson at San Patricio, set out from Matamoros to meet them. He and approximately 700 men arrived at the Irish town at three o'clock on the morning of February 27.[1] Immediately, and in the midst of a driving rainstorm, he ordered an assault. Johnson and his men were the only occupants of the town; Grant and his men were away searching for horses. The defenders were overcome. Nine or 10 of the Texans were killed in the fighting, and, except for Johnson and a few who escaped, the rest were captured. Grant's men were surprised and killed on March 2 at Agua Dulce Creek. Of the men taken at San Patricio, Father Molloy of San Patricio was able to save 18 from execution. These were sent as prisoners to Mexico.

Dawn at the Alamo *by Harry Arthur McArdle*

Santa Anna's advance units had reached San Antonio on February 23, and the Texans there retired with Colonel William Barret Travis into the Alamo. From behind its walls, approximately 188 defenders hurled defiance at the massing thousands of the dictator's army. The story of their stand is well known: When they refused the demand to surrender, the order of "no quarter" was given. The Alamo was taken on March 6, 1836. All the defenders died. Among them were 12 Irish-born men and an additional 14 bearing Irish surnames. Eight or nine of those in the old mission were settlers from the Irish colonies to the south.[2] Three of the Irish-born were from Gonzales—the only Texas community to answer Travis's plea for help.

After the fall of the Alamo, Santa Anna continued eastward in search of Sam Houston's retreating army—and to his defeat at San Jacinto.

Meanwhile, the abandoned property of the San Patricio Irish had been occupied for almost two weeks by Urrea's men. His troops now numbered an estimated 1,000.[3] On March 13 he began the advance to Goliad but turned aside to Refugio when he heard it had been occupied by some of Fannin's men.

Known Irish-born Men Who Died at the Alamo

Samuel E. Burns, Andrew Duvalt, Robert Evans, Joseph M. Hawkins, William D. Jackson, Edward McCafferty, James McGee, Robert McKinney, James Nowlan, Jackson J. Rusk, Burke Trammel, and William B. Ward.[4]

The greater part of the militia of the Irish colonies was in Hugh McDonald Frazer's and Ira Westover's companies with Fannin at Goliad.[5] Many of the families had been moved to places of safety, but there were still a few in the Refugio area. Without teams or wagons and with no militia to protect them, the women and children sought help from Goliad. Fannin dispatched Captain Amon King and a detachment that included several Irish volunteers to escort the families and their possessions to the protection of Refugio Mission. The flight of the families under escort was noted by advance units of Urrea's cavalry. The Mexican horsemen pursued the lumbering oxcarts, but the Texans reached the stout walls of the mission safely. However, they were in danger of being entrapped there, and King dispatched young Thomas John O'Brien to Goliad with news of the predicament. Fannin then sent William Ward and part of his Georgia battalion to relieve King.[6]

Ward arrived at Refugio on March 13. Bickering between Ward and King and a misconception of the strength of Urrea's forces resulted in a division in the command. King and his men left the mission in one direction, while Ward's men took another. The latter, realizing the strength of Urrea's still-assembling forces, returned. They alone faced the mounting attacks of the Mexican army. When, on March 14, Urrea launched his final assault, he found the mission occupied by eight women, five or six children, and three wounded men. Ward and his men had slipped away the previous night. They were captured on March 22 and marched to Goliad.[7]

King and his men were captured near Refugio on or about March 15. All but three were shot within sight of the women and children at the mission, and their bodies were left on the prairie. Nearby lay the body of a messenger from Fannin at Goliad, James Murphy, who had attempted to reach the Refugio Mission through the Mexican lines.[8]

On March 16, at Urrea's orders, a Mexican detachment under Colonel Rafael de la Vara occupied Copano. Thus, the Irish colonies were sealed off.[9]

On March 19 Urrea's advance units were already before Goliad, and the vacillating Fannin finally left that place to join Houston's army to the east. After a few hours, he halted his men on the open prairie near Coleto Creek and was there surrounded and taken by the Mexicans after a bloody battle. Among 10 Texans killed or wounded were John Kelly, Alfred Dorsey, and William Quinn.[10] A total of 284 men of Fannin's command were marched back to Goliad. There they were joined by Ward's 80 men captured near Victoria—that town had been taken by Urrea on March 21—and by others from Refugio. In all, the total number of prisoners at Goliad is estimated at 407.

On direct orders from Santa Anna on March 27, the prisoners were marched out of the fort in three groups and shot down on the open prairie. Some 28 escaped into nearby woods, and 20 were spared because of help from Mexican friends or, as in the case of doctors, because their skills were needed.

At least 47 Celtic surnames appear on the list of those killed at Coleto and Goliad. Many more than those mentioned were probably Irish-born, since the New Orleans Greys were part of Fannin's command and there were Irish-born volunteers in that unit. The escape of Nicholas and John Fagan, Edward Perry, Anthony and John Sidick, and James Byrnes was arranged by Mexican Captain Carlos de la Garza. These men were all his neighbors, living near him on the San Antonio River. Nicholas Fagan was in the line of those being herded outside for execution, when some of de la Garza's rancheros laid a quarter side of beef on his shoulders to hide his identity so he could walk away from the line. He escaped through a nearby orchard. After the shooting he came back and found William L. Hunter still alive. He carried him to Manehuila Creek, where they hid from Mexican patrols combing the area for those who had escaped.

Andrew Boyle of San Patricio was saved by a Mexican officer who had been treated hospitably by Boyle's brother and sister.[11]

San Patricio and Refugio Irish Who Died at Coleto Creek and Goliad

Matthew Byrne, George W. Cash, Alfred Dorsey, John Fadden, Lewis Gates, Edward Garner, John Gleeson, John James, John Kelly, John McGloin, Dennis McGowan, Patrick Neven, Thomas Quinn, William Quinn, Thomas Quirk, and Edward Ryan.[12]

None Paid a Greater Price

In terms of lives sacrificed, property lost, and land despoiled, none gave more to Texas independence than the Irish colonists of San Patricio, Refugio, and Victoria. When they espoused the Texas cause, they knew they would bear the brunt of the conflict. Their colonial area was a crossroads of battle.

The Texans attempted to hold a western front on a line running generally southeast from San Antonio to the Gulf. The tide of conflict ebbed and flowed across this line, washing over the lands of the Irish colonists. Except for the Battle of San Jacinto—fought just east of present-day Houston—most of the military operations were conducted west of the Guadalupe and south of a line running westward from Gonzales to San Antonio. The towns of San Patricio, Refugio, and Victoria were burned. Property and homes were destroyed and livestock driven off. The areas were almost depopulated.

The colonists of this area had provisioned and supplied the volunteers who gathered there in 1835 and 1836. Two gunsmiths of Refugio, Edmund Quirk and Antoine Sayle, repaired and maintained the guns of the men of Fannin's command. Merchants Henry Foley, Martin Power, and John Dunn furnished large quantities of dry goods and clothing. Nicholas Fagan placed his whole corn crop and several hundred head of cattle at the disposal of the Texans. Foodstuffs were provided and transported by John Fagan, Peter Hynes, Edward McDonough, John J. Linn, and five Mexican colonists of the area.[1]

Sending their wives and children to safety in the eastern colonies and in Louisiana, most of the men joined the Texan volunteers and regular army units that took the field against Santa Anna.

These colonists would continue to pay for some years after San Jacinto. The Texas upheaval had attracted to the area a number of men whose only purpose was to plunder. In the patriots' absence, their deserted homes were looted and their livestock driven off.

In her "Reminiscences," Mrs. Annie Fagan Teal tells of well-mounted men causing panic by riding through the country shouting that the Mexicans and Indians were coming, looting and killing on the way. Leaving behind all their possessions, she and the women and children of other families headed east in headlong flight. On the way they were accosted by a band of men who took their weapons, leaving them defenseless. When she returned after San Jacinto, plunderers had driven off all but one cow of the large herds of Nicholas Fagan, Peter Teal, and Edward McDonough. The robbers were still at work, and she saw load after load of elegantly carved mahogany furniture being taken from the deserted homes of rich Mexicans.[2] Pillage and murder were to continue in this part of the country for some years. Indians, Anglo-American and Mexican bandits, the Mexican army, and even the frontier-based Texas army would plague this area through the late 1830's and 1840's.

The infant Republic of Texas was, after San Jacinto, inundated by waves of volunteers from the United States. The army that had fought at San Jacinto had been composed mainly of colonists. Most of the survivors had gone back to their farms and ranches. The new army was made up of latecomers with, as one historian noted, neither rights nor property in Texas to defend.[3] It became a problem to the government, at times even a threat to public order and stability. At one time some members of the rebellious army had planned to arrest Texas President David G. Burnet and seize the government.[4] The authorities considered it safer to move this rebellious group far from the seat of government and closer to the Mexican border. The army was sent west to the frontier, which was then San Antonio and the area of the Irish colonies.

Plagued by a money shortage, the authorities were unable to pay or provision the soldiers, and they started foraging on the neighboring ranches. Abuses by the army prompted the government, in August of 1836, to declare any unauthorized seizure of property a felony.[5] Some of the soldiers, after discharge, remained in the area and continued stealing for their private profit. Much of the stolen property came from the homes of men who had fought for and helped secure Texas independence.

In October of 1836, a proposal was made to the Texas government that all cattle, stock, and other provisions between the Guadalupe and the Rio Grande be moved or destroyed so that nothing would be left for an invading Mexican army. It was also proposed that settlers on the Nueces and San Antonio rivers be compelled to move either east or west,[6] but such proposals were not accepted by the Irish colonists. They would have lost everything that they had worked so hard to build.

Depredations continued, and, in 1839, the Third Congress of the Republic enacted laws that made the stealing or driving off of cattle not belonging to the drover a felony punishable by death.[7] It was one matter, however, to enact laws and quite another to enforce them. In 1842 Refugio settlers were still complaining of troops seizing cows and young calves.[8]

The San Patricio area was suffering in the same way. In early 1842 the government ordered Major Thomas Casey of the Department of War and Marine to relieve the officer in command of the troops on the Nueces near Corpus Christi. In defiance of their government, the troops refused to accept Casey.[9] In June of that same year, the same soldiers were reported as imprisoning traders and seizing and dividing their goods.[10] The Irish colonies would have been better off without those troops which preyed upon them but showed themselves particularly inept in defending the area against Indian raids, desperados, and the incursions of the Mexican army.

Another scourge was the looting freebooters who roamed the area, driving off livestock and robbing merchants. They became so powerful that, in the 1840's, they operated openly and murdered in broad daylight in front of scores of witnesses. They instituted such a reign of terror that no witness, if he valued his life, would testify against them.[11] The Nueces settlements, farthest removed from the center of government, were subject to continual raids and harassment, and the Nueces River became known as the "deadline for sheriffs."

Added to these problems were Indian raids, familiar to the Irish colonists from their first days in Texas. When the San Patricio colonists arrived at Refugio in late 1829, the newcomers were duly noted by Indian scouts. The outsiders were accosted by the Lipans, who demanded gifts. A hastily organized militia under Captain John Kelly and the firing of a cannon discouraged the warriors. They apparently respected the show of strength because, explaining they had to make camp for the night, they sauntered off.[12]

The John Corrigan family on Aransas Creek had to leave their home several times when threatened by hostile Indians. An account is given of how once, when Mrs. Ellen O'Toole Corrigan was alone, Indians came, killed the dog, and stole her saddle pony, which was tied near the door of the house. At another time a Jerome Murphy, on his way from Victoria to San Patricio, stopped at a creek near the Corrigan home to prepare dinner. His meal was interrupted by the sight of a band of Indians riding toward him. He ran to the Corrigan house, leaving his horse, cooking utensils, and the remains of his meal. Mrs. Corrigan tried to prevail on him to take her horse and ride to warn her husband, who was in the nearby woods cutting timber. He refused, and the dauntless woman tied a red bandana around her head and rode out herself to alert her husband. She

Mary Heffernan Riggs, daughter of John Heffernan, was about 15 at the time of the Heffernan massacre. Her reminiscence is the only narrative account of the tragedy.

found him, and they rode back to the house, where Murphy and some Rangers who had ridden up were engaging the Indians.[13]

The family of James Heffernan (later spelled Hefferman) was not as lucky as the Corrigans. In 1835 the Indians, in a surprise attack on their home on Poesta Creek, massacred the entire family. Their remains were found a few days later. The three men—James and his brother, John, and a cousin named Ryan—were apparently at work in the fields unaware of danger. Their bodies were found there. Those of Mrs. Heffernan and the children were found at the house.[14] The county courthouse at Beeville is said to stand on the site of this massacre.

On February 16, 1836, Indians stole all the horses of the San Patricio settlement and killed three people on the west side of the Nueces near the town.[15]

The Indians, of course, were equally taken aback by the settlers. The land formerly theirs was now being taken over by people having a very different conception of "ownership." To the colonials, naturally, it was the Indians who were "problems."

The Karankawas of the coast region had always been a problem to the settlers, but their raids were nothing compared to the ferocity of the well-

The Pajarita de Sangre, once a favorite place of ambush along a road from the coast to Goliad

Ellen O'Toole Corrigan

organized Comanches. In 1838 a messenger rode south from San Antonio to warn Colonel Power that a force of 900 Indians was coming down on the colony. Two bands of Comanches rode south that year—one coming down the San Antonio River, the other down Aransas Creek. Irish and Mexican colonists banded under James Power to meet them. A bloody clash ensued in which a couple of colonists were killed.[16]

In those days, as today, certain locations acquired reputations because of occurrences there. One such was Pajarita de Sangre (Bloody Little Bird) on the San Antonio River eight miles southeast of the site of the Battle of Coleto. It was a point of timber in which, over the years, had occurred several robberies and murders. The death there of an Indian chief, Little Bird, had given it its name.

It almost lived up to its name of "bloody" for John Fagan, son of Nicholas Fagan. Unaware that Indians were in the area, he and a Joe Howard were riding from the Peter Teal home to Goliad and passing through the Pajarita de Sangre. Howard was about 150 yards ahead of Fagan, and, as he topped a hill, the Indians rode from the chaparral and surrounded and killed him. Fagan wheeled and rode for his life. His horse was beginning to fail, and he headed for the thick timber. There he abandoned the horse but escaped in the dense undergrowth and made his way to the Teal home. Informing the family of Howard's fate and that Indians were coming, he and Teal penned some of the horses and milk cows and prepared for a siege. With Indian war cries heralding the approach of the warriors, they securely bolted the doors and windows of the house and opened the rifle portholes. The two men, each behind a flint-and-steel rifle, waited for the charge. Mrs. Annie Fagan Teal, her two-year-old clinging to her skirts, stood by the bed on which the ammunition had been spread, ready to reload as fast as the men could shoot.

For about two hours, not daring to charge, the Indians circled the house. At one point a warrior riding Howard's horse came within rifle range. Fagan wanted to shoot but was prevented by Teal's admonition not to be ". . . caught with an empty gun, but withhold your fire until they charge the house."

The attackers were distracted by the sight of a Mexican boy coming up the flats riding one horse and leading another. His capture occurred in full view of those in the house. Another Mexican, coming from the direction of Victoria,

Capt. Henry Scott, Refugio County rancher, witnessed two periods of lawlessness. As a boy after the Texas Revolution, Scott rode with minutemen led by his father, John Scott. During a similar time of social unrest following the Civil War, Henry Scott formed his own minuteman company. In A Vaquero of the Brush Country *by J. Frank Dobie, Capt. Henry Scott was remembered as a leader of "sound judgement and strict honor."*

was their next victim. Again those in the house watched, helpless as the Mexican, dodging in the tall grass, sought to evade his pursuers. He fell, riddled by 15 arrows. Apparently satisfied, the Indians then rode away.[17]

Early in 1840 the Lipans raided the ranches on the coast and were pursued to the Rio Grande by a group of colonists. Ten-year-old Henry Scott was in the party led by his father, John Scott. At the river the Indians ambushed the white men, killing the elder Scott and several others. Henry was captured and taken across the Rio Grande but later escaped and returned to his family at Refugio.[18]

In August of that same year, the "Great Comanche Raid" occurred, in which at least 15 colonists were killed, four women and three children were taken captive, and the town of Linnville was plundered and burned. The raid appears to have been a reprisal for the killing of 12 chiefs and 23 warriors, women, and children at the Council House Fight of March 19, 1840, in San Antonio.

On August 5 an estimated 1,000 Comanches swept like a scythe of death and destruction from east of Gonzales and down the San Antonio River. They encircled Victoria on August 6 but did not attack. So sudden was their appearance that some ranchers were caught in the town, their homes and families unprotected. One band attacked the Johnson [Johnstone] Gilleland place, murdering Mr. and Mrs. Gilleland and taking the two children captive. Nicholas Fagan, whose ranch was a short distance away, heard the shots, and he and others pursued the raiders. They caught up with them about 12 miles away. The Indians fled, leaving the children for dead. They had run a lance through the little boy and struck his seven-year-old sister on the head. Fagan had the children's wounds attended to, and they recovered.[19]

Meanwhile the main band descended on Linnville. The residents there fled to the safety of a barge in the bay and watched the Indians plunder and burn the town. One of them, Judge John Hays, unable to control his indignation and anger, announced that he would teach the "red devils a lesson." Snatching up a rifle, he jumped into the shallow waters of the bay and stalked onto the beach, where he stood waiting for an Indian to come within range. The Indians, who had a great respect for madmen, must have thought him deranged, for they simply ignored him and did not ride into range. Judge Hays later returned to the barge—where he discovered the rifle was not loaded.

Meanwhile, local settlers had been organizing. When the Indians started northward with their loot and captives, the colonists overtook them south of Austin at Plum Creek near present-day Lockhart. Indians often killed their captives rather than surrender them alive or let them impede their flight. In this case, captive Mrs. H.O. Watts of Linnville was lucky.

Seeing that flight was inevitable, a Comanche brave took deadly aim at Mrs. Watts. His arrow flew straight and true and should have transfixed the woman's body. He was surprised to see the arrow hit the target and bounce off. This was strong "medicine" indeed! Bewildered, he wheeled his horse and followed his companions in flight. Mrs. Watts was thankful that she had been wearing a corset with wide steel stays.[20]

Indian depredations continued for many years. One historian notes that "practically every settler was visited by them." As late as 1846, James Hart, son of Timothy Hart, was captured by Indians. His release was later effected by Indian agents.[21] In 1850 several bands of Comanches raided the Thomas ranch. Two girls were away from the protection of the house and were taken captive. The last Indian fight in that area was in 1852 with Karankawas at Hynes Spring. A group of Irish settlers, under the leadership of Refugio County Sheriff John Hynes, so completely routed the Indians that the remnants of the Karankawa tribe left Texas for Mexico.[22]

After San Jacinto, Mexican troops were ordered to retire across the Rio Grande. These made up the greater part of the thousands that Santa Anna had brought with him to Texas, since he had only a small contingent with him when he was defeated and captured near Buffalo Bayou. General Vicente Filisola succeeded to the command and began the retreat with an army in need of provisions. On finding no supplies at Victoria, he marched for Goliad.

The other Mexican general, José Urrea, occupied Refugio. In the third week of May, both contingents started for Matamoros via San Patricio. Without supplies, the army was forced to live off the country, and the homes and livestock of the Irish colonists were again plundered for what little remained.

San Patricio, according to John McMullen, had 500 inhabitants at the beginning of the Texas War of Independence but was abandoned and burned at the end. He reports having upwards of 1,300 head of cattle in November 1835, but all had been driven off "by one or the other party." His books were destroyed, his private arms were taken, and everything he had was ruined or plundered.[23]

For the next few years, this was to be the story of the Irish colonies. The Irish of San Patricio were forced so often from their homes by Indians or bandits that some would eventually abandon them and set up towns elsewhere in Texas.

On a warm day in March 1838, James Power and Walter Lambert were working in the Power store at Aransas City on Live Oak Point. Power glanced out and noticed a large band of horsemen riding in the direction of the settlement. "Look like traders," he mused and went back to his work. He heard the men stop outside, dismount, and, spurs jangling, cross the wooden porch. Turning to greet them as they entered, he found himself looking down the barrel of a rifle in the hands of de los Santos, the leader. While Power and Lambert were held at gunpoint and Mrs. Tomasa de la Portilla Power looked on, the bandits proceeded to loot the store and the Power home. Taking what they could conveniently carry, they forced Power to accompany them. Before leaving, Power instructed Lambert and Mrs. Power to close the business and lock the doors.

The bandits had no sooner departed when a second gang came and demanded entrance. Lambert prepared to resist them by force, but Mrs. Power, fearing for

Aransas City on Live Oak Point, where James Power's store and residence were located; painting by W.H. Sandusky, 1842

the safety of her husband, restrained him. This group remained for three days, terrorizing Mrs. Power, the children, and the neighbors. When they left, they took personal goods, a number of cattle, and several oxen. Meanwhile, Power was taken to Matamoros, where he was kept prisoner for five months.[24]

In 1839 Mexican General Antonio Canales, who was leading a revolt against Santa Anna, made his headquarters at Fort Lipantitlán across from the town of San Patricio. The Texas government made no overt attempt to dislodge him, and the people of San Patricio were under the guns of a Mexican rebel army.

After San Jacinto the war was not over. Raids along the coast in May 1841 by Mexican troops supposedly looking for contraband prompted the organization of a company of San Patricio Rangers. The Mexican patrols were under the command of Agatón Quiñones. On July 4 a Mexican force swept down on Padre Island and took Phillip Dimmitt, the former commander at Goliad, and three others as prisoners to Mexico. Perhaps anticipating the fate prepared for him, this noted leader took his own life by an overdose of morphine.

On September 1, in an incident known as the "sacking of Refugio," Quiñones's troops took Refugio, captured every man except one, and looted the

Michael Whelan, one of the volunteers who participated in the Battle of the Nueces near San Patricio in 1841, came to Refugio from County Wexford in 1839 and became a cattleman on the free range. Perhaps the unstable conditions on the frontier of the new republic were the reason Whelan's wife and children remained in Ireland until after Texas became a state.

town. Henry Ryals barricaded himself in his house and defied the attackers. Unable to dislodge him, they promised him his life if he surrendered. Ryals did so, and the prisoners, hands bound in front, were tied to the tails of the Mexicans' horses. At a brisk trot, the men were dragged to a point named Burke's Hollow, six miles south of the town. Here Henry Ryals ". . . the only colonist who had shown fight, was strung to the limb of a tree and riddled with bullets." The rest of the prisoners, including James Power, were taken to Mexico, where they were released through the intercession of James Hewetson, Power's former partner, who was living in Mexico.[25]

Neither Santa Anna, back in power, nor the Mexican government considered San Jacinto the end of hostilities.[26] General Rafael Vásquez, commanding a regular Mexican army, invaded Texas in February 1842 and sent a 200-man detachment under Captain Ramón Valera to capture Goliad, Refugio, and San Patricio. Troops under Captain José Manuel Gonzales were to move on the colonies from the west. Goliad was taken on March 4. On the same day that Vásquez entered San Antonio, March 6, Valera's troops took Refugio. The Texan troops were away from the town at the time and were reported to be near San Patricio. Meanwhile, on March 7, 10 men from San Patricio were encamped at Rock Pass, where they were attacked by Gonzales. Four were killed and the rest captured.[27] Valera moved on San Patricio, and 200 Texans were trapped between his force and that of Gonzales coming from the west. A number of Texans were killed. Vásquez then retired with his forces to Mexico.[28]

Three and a half months later, another Mexican army threatened San Patricio. This one was under the command of General Canales, who, unsuccessful in his revolt against Santa Anna, had joined the Mexican dictator. Nine miles west of San Patricio, his force of 700 men was met on July 6 by a much smaller group of Texans. Both sides claimed victory in the Battle of the Nueces.

Harrassed by the pillaging units of a Texas army that was supposed to protect them and bearing the burden of Mexican raids and the uncurbed lawlessness of the frontier, the settlers of the Irish colonies were understandably resentful of those in the east who controlled the government. They felt they were being sacrificed as a buffer zone to the welfare of other settlements far from the frontier. The resentment found voice in the comments of one Refugio resident to his representative at Austin:

". . . a portion of the population . . . too cowardly to make pioneers—are most strongly represented in Congress—whose interest is to help us back until they can realize a profit on their investment fast—then we shall be too poor to prevent them from running over us—when the danger is all over—but it is our duty—stand to our arms and interest—give them all the trouble you can in their opposition to the West . . . we have nothing to expect from . . . the patriotism of the East who feel themselves secure from the troubles of this country."[29]

Irish at the Battle of the Nueces

Patrick Bray; James Burke; Michael Cahill; Jeremiah Findlay; Edward Fitzgerald; John FitzSimmons; James, John, and Michael Fox; Walter Lambert; Edward Linn; Patrick Mahan; Morgan O'Brien; Thomas O'Connor; Daniel O'Driscoll; James Power; and Henry and Michael Whelan.[30]

The Irish of Victoria

The Victoria colony of empresario Martín de León, although composed mostly of Mexican settlers, contained a number of Irish families.

One of the most prominent Irishmen there was John J. Linn, born in County Antrim, Ireland, in 1798. His father, a college professor, was active in the unsuccessful Irish uprising of that year and fled to America to avoid arrest. He obtained a teaching position in Poughkeepsie, New York, and was joined by his family in 1800.

John J. Linn came south in 1822 and located in New Orleans, where he went into the mercantile business.[1] He was one of a number of American traders dealing in contraband, who sold goods to Mexicans on the Texas coast for transshipment to Mexico across the Rio Grande. By his own account, he landed at least two cargoes of contraband goods in the area of present-day Corpus Christi.[2] At one time he probably sold smuggled goods to the colonists at Victoria.

As a settler in Victoria, he was entitled to a league of land—which he never claimed—and a town lot, where he constructed a house to which he brought his mother, father, and younger brother in 1831. In 1834 he brought his New Orleans bride to Texas. He built a successful merchandising business and warehouse in town, and by 1836 he was receiving goods from New Orleans by sea on a somewhat regular schedule. This fact was to prove valuable for the supply of Texas troops in the war with Mexico.

An enthusiastic supporter of the Texas cause, Linn had been named a delegate to the San Felipe Consultation—a meeting of colonists to decide Texas's

John J. Linn

attitude toward Santa Anna's assumption of dictatorial powers. He participated in the capture of Goliad in October 1835 and in the Battle of Lipantitlán and was quartermaster for Fannin's command. When Mexican troops overran the Irish colonies, he organized the citizens of Victoria for evacuation. On Fannin's appeal for wagons and oxen to remove the garrison from Goliad, Linn reluctantly sent him the 20 yoke of oxen the Victoria citizens had assembled for their own transport.[3] As a result some of the citizens were trapped in the town.

John Linn left Victoria with his family and only the provisions they

John J. Linn's residence (foreground) *shortly before demolition, Victoria, 1893*

could carry on St. Patrick's Day, March 17, 1836, and headed for Lavaca Bay, where he expected to find his supply-laden boat. On the way he met de León, who told him that he had encountered Houston in full retreat. Leaving his family in de León's care, Linn rode out to join Houston's army just as an advance guard of General Urrea's Mexican army rode into the de León ranch.[4]

Linn caught up with Houston before San Jacinto but was sent to Galveston to receive a shipload of supplies consigned to him. He transferred the supplies to a small river steamer and delivered flour, coffee, sugar, soap, and lead to the men at San Jacinto. When Texas General Thomas J. Rusk and his men were dispatched, after San Jacinto, to follow up and ensure that Santa Anna's armies left Texas, Linn accompanied them as far as Victoria. John J. Linn served as a member of the Republic of Texas House of Representatives and was elected the first mayor of Victoria when that town was chartered as a municipality in 1839. A son, John, died in Confederate service in 1862.[5]

Among the Irish living in Victoria, and trapped there when Urrea's men occupied it on March 21, 1836, were the Quinns and the Haleys. Mrs. Elizabeth McAnulty Owens, whose widowed mother had married James Quinn, left an account of those days. She was nine years old at the time. Her mother and stepfather were one of the 53 families first brought by McMullen-McGloin in 1829. They had stayed at the Refugio Mission when the others went to the Nueces River. In 1835 Quinn obtained a league of land in the de León Colony.

When hostilities broke out ". . . Placido Benavides organized a company to join Fannin at La Bahía, every man going who could shoulder a gun. James Quinn was one of these. His brother William, having been one of the signers of the Goliad Declaration of Independence, was already with Fannin's men. The women met at the home of Mrs. John Linn to mold bullets and in other ways to assist the cause espoused by their husbands."

As Urrea advanced across the Irish colonies and Fannin started his retreat, James Quinn was one of the colonists sent home to remove his family from the path of the invading Mexican army. Unable to find means of transport, the Quinns were compelled to stay in Victoria.

Mrs. Owens relates that "During the assault upon Fannin the cannonading could be plainly heard in Victoria." No doubt James Quinn's thoughts were of his brother and friends who were with the Texans. He did not know until later that William was one of those killed on that grassy plain near Coleto Creek.

While the guns were still roaring, the apprehensive family was startled by the arrival of a courier from the east with a message for Fannin. Knowing it was useless to go on, he took refuge with the Quinns and stayed to bring them up to date on events. Darkness had closed in, and, as he talked, Elizabeth ". . . sat on the hearth holding a candle in the chimney so the light could not be seen."

Suddenly a shot rang out in the town, causing the courier to stop in mid-sentence. He leaped from his seat, vaulted to his horse, and rode away into the

Elizabeth McAnulty Owens, whose reminiscences provide a valuable record of events in Victoria from the 1830's to the 1860's

Thomas Marion O'Connor, Victoria cattleman for whom Port O'Connor was named

darkness. "He was overtaken and killed near the site of the present Evergreen Cemetery." Mexican advance units were in Victoria.

As described by Mrs. Owens, "The invading Mexican army reached Victoria in great glory, blowing their bugles, sounding their drums and parading the streets." One of the officers came to Mrs. Quinn's door, walked in, and took possession of one of the front rooms. "The colonel of the Mexican army resided in the Linn home, . . ." which was abandoned. The Mexican troops occupied the town until after the battle of San Jacinto.

Even after San Jacinto, the threat of Mexican invasion caused apprehension in western Texas communities. Frayed nerves—and poor eyesight—resulted in the burning of Victoria in the fall of 1837. What appeared to be the Mexican army materialized on one of the hills beyond the town. The occupying Texas army, under Colonel James W. Tinsley, prepared feverishly for defense. The colonel ordered all houses burned except those facing the square. These were to be the line of defense. With all in readiness, the defenders awaited the "assault." The "army" turned out to be a herd of deer. The situation was not humorous to people like the Quinns who had to find shelter for the winter in the church.[6]

Patrick Mahan, an 1832 Irish settler of Victoria, was a member of the Mier Expedition captured by the Mexicans in 1842. He drew a black bean in the lottery of death conducted by the Mexican commander and was one of those who was shot.

In spite of the decade of war, Irish settlers continued to come to the Victoria area. In 1846 Irish-born Peter Byrne arrived in Texas and established a ranch in

Victoria County. Another Byrne who settled nearby was, as far as is known, no relation. This was James W. Byrne, who purchased, in 1838, extensive acreage on the Lamar Peninsula across St. Charles Bay from the present Aransas National Wildlife Refuge. He was born in Ireland and grew up in France, whence his family had fled after the 1798 Uprising. He served as county clerk of Refugio in 1839 and 1840, then represented the Refugio District in the 5th, 6th, and 7th Senates of the Texas Republic.[7]

Mrs. Brigid Eagan opened a plantation 10 miles south of Victoria in 1846. Her nephew, Irish-born Patrick Hughes, arrived in 1852 and became one of the most prominent ranchers in the area. He served as a Confederate officer.

Commercial establishments often were lucrative operations in early Texas and attracted many who came to Victoria. Irish-born Andrew Oliver came to the city in 1846 and opened a store on Main Street. In the mid-1860's, he went into business in San Antonio but in 1868 returned to Victoria, where his store became known for the most extensive and choice stock of Irish linens.

Michael O'Keefe had come to Texas from Ireland via New Orleans in 1851 and, as a carpenter, established a prosperous trade in Victoria. John Mahon, another native of Ireland, opened a dry goods store in the town in 1865. He served terms as mayor, alderman, and county commissioner.[8]

During the Civil War, Irish settlers from Victoria served in the 6th Texas Infantry and in the 13th Texas Cavalry.[9]

Almost every community has its share of eccentrics. The Irish community of Victoria was no exception. Stories are told of one O'Reagan, who lived there in the Civil War era. An ambrotypist, practitioner of an old style of photography,

John Mahon (left) in his dry goods store, Victoria, c. 1890

Patrick Hughes

he was seemingly quite out of place in that frontier community. He wore his hair long, disregarded his dress and appearance, and was given to freely expressing his opinions and thoughts even when opposed to local convention and political belief. A pro-Unionist, he let it be known that he was "secretly" working on a machine by which he intended to reach the blockading Union squadron in the Gulf.

Once, O'Reagan and three friends were sitting up with an invalid who was in the last stages of consumption. The friends were fortifying themselves against the patient's impending demise, and, by the time he expired, they had consumed enough "red-eye" to insulate themselves against the awful reality. With proper—if somewhat befuddled—solemnity, they closed the eyes of the corpse, placed coins on the eyelids, and were about to take their sad and lurching departure, when O'Reagan made a suggestion. He proposed that "in the interest of science," he apply a galvanic battery to the corpse's spinal column. Without quite comprehending how, the others agreed that science must be served. They were not, however, prepared for the effects.

The current was applied as they watched with detached and almost sleepy disinterest. Their expressions changed to frozen, wide-eyed horror as the body began to twitch. The nervous twitching increased, but, with hearts pounding and scalps tingling, they were rooted to the spot. Suddenly the corpse's eyes flew open, flipping the coins to the floor. The spell was broken, and there was a mad rush for the door. O'Reagan was unperturbed by all this and only seemed disappointed that the corpse did not get up and walk. The others agreed afterward that it was a most sobering experience.

Disturbances in the Irish Colonies 1835-1852

Listed below are the Mexican and some of the Indian raids on the Irish colonies. No attempt has been made to catalog seizures of stock by the Texas army or the murders, stock thefts, and plundering by desperadoes from both sides of the border.

Sept. 1835	General Cos lands with Mexican troops at Copano.
Oct. 2, 1835	Cos leaves detachment occupying fort at Goliad.
Oct. 10, 1835	Colonists capture fort at Goliad.
Nov. 3, 1835	Colonists capture Fort Lipantitlán.
Nov. 4, 1835	Colonists defeat Mexicans in battle on Nueces River.
Feb. 1836	Indians attack Corrigan ranch, massacre Heffernan family.
Feb. 27, 1836	General Urrea's forces assault and take San Patricio.
Mar. 2, 1836	Mexicans surprise Grant's Texans at Agua Dulce Creek.
Mar. 13, 1836	Urrea advances on Goliad, attacks mission at Refugio.
Mar. 14, 1836	Mexicans capture Refugio Mission.
Mar. 15, 1836	King and his Texans are captured and shot at Refugio.

Mar. 16, 1836	Copano is occupied by Mexican detachment under de la Vara.
Mar. 19, 1836	Fannin retreats from Goliad, surrounded by Mexicans at Coleto Creek.
Mar. 20, 1836	Fannin surrenders at Coleto Creek.
Mar. 21, 1836	Urrea's troops occupy Victoria.
Mar. 22, 1836	Ward and 80 men are captured near Victoria, marched to Goliad.
Mar. 27, 1836	Goliad Massacre—Many Irish colonists die.
May 1836	Mexican army retreats; Texas army occupies Irish colonies.
Mar. 1838	De los Santos's Mexican soldier-bandits plunder Power home and store, take him prisoner. A second bandit gang plunders Aransas City.
1839	Mexican rebel general, Canales, occupies Fort Lipantitlán.
Early 1840	Lipan Indians raid coastal ranches.
Aug. 1840	Great Comanche Raid—Linnville is burned; ranches on San Antonio River are attacked.
May 1841	Quiñones's Mexican troops raid Padre Island; Dimmitt and others are captured.
Sept. 1841	Quiñones's troops sack Refugio, murder Henry Ryals, take Power and five others as prisoners to Mexico.
Feb. 1842	Mexican General Vásquez invades Texas.
Mar. 4, 1842	Goliad is taken by Valera's contingent.
Mar. 6, 1842	Refugio is occupied by Valera's troops.
Mar. 7, 1842	Gonzales's troops kill four San Patricians, capture six.
Mar. 1842	Texans are trapped at San Patricio between Gonzales's and Valera's men.
July 6, 1842	Texans repel Canales's Mexican troops at San Patricio.
1846	Indian raids—James Hart is captured.
1852	Last Indian fight, with Karankawas, who leave Texas for Mexico.

Texas Irish and the Civil War

When Texas entered the Confederacy, the Irish of Texas supported their state. Eighteen Irish settlers had signed the 1861 Ordinance of Secession. Irish names graced the rolls of the Texas regiments that fought the bitter campaigns of the Civil War.[1] Additionally, in Texas itself, there were two brilliant exploits involving the Texas Irish.

In late 1862 Union forces attacked and captured the city of Galveston. Confederate General John Magruder, intent on recapturing the city and destroying the blockading Union squadron, ordered the steamer *Bayou City* to the relief of Galveston. With a newly mounted gun and protected by bales of cotton, this prewar passenger and freight carrier joined another Confederate steamer, the *Neptune*. They were to attack the Federal gunboats while Confederate land forces assaulted the city.

In the dull gray dawn of January 1, 1863, Confederate land batteries started pounding the entrenched Federals in the city. The land batteries were soon silenced by the Union gunboats *Harriet Lane* and *Owasco*. Waves of gray-clad Texas infantry rolled toward the city walls but, without the covering fire of their artillery, were driven back by the barricaded Northern troops. The land attack had failed.

Meanwhile, the two Confederate vessels crossed Galveston Bay and attacked the Federal ships. The *Neptune* was hit, and it sank, leaving the other Confederate steamer to face the enemy alone. Her gun had been damaged in the first

The Battle of Galveston, January 1, 1863, with the Harriet Lane *(center) shortly before it was captured by the Confederates*

three salvos, and, without firepower, there was only one course open to the pilot of the *Bayou City*. The larger Union gunboat, *Harriet Lane*, had to be boarded or sunk.

Ignoring the concentrated enemy fire that he was now unable to return, the Texan pilot steered straight for the enemy vessel, ramming her and so entangling the two vessels that the *Harriet Lane* was boarded and captured. Stripped of the supporting naval squadron, the Federal garrison at Galveston surrendered, and the remaining Union gunboats sailed away under a white flag. Galveston had been recaptured for the Confederacy.

The intrepid pilot of the *Bayou City* was Michael McCormick, Irish-born son of the Peggy McCormick on whose land the Battle of San Jacinto had been fought 27 years before.[2]

Among the men who stormed aboard the *Harriet Lane* from the deck of the *Bayou City* was Peter Fagan, son of Nicholas Fagan of the Refugio Colony. Peter, at 18, had enlisted in Company C of Sibley's Brigade, 4th Texas Cavalry. He had served at the Battle of Glorieta in New Mexico and had also fought at the Battles of Palo Alto and Val Verde The men marched back afoot from El Paso to San Antonio. After that experience Fagan "vowed that he would never again be without a good horse." (He wasn't. His descendants still raise quality horseflesh on the old ranch.) After a short rest in San Antonio, his company was mustered at Houston and there put aboard the *Bayou City*. After the Battle of Galveston

Dick Dowling

Bay, his unit was ordered to Louisiana, where Fagan participated in the Battles of Mansfield, Pleasant Hill, Blair's Landing, and Jenkins Ferry.[3]

Also participating in the recapture of Galveston was an Irishman who, with his fellow countrymen of Houston and Galveston, was to write another brilliant page in Texas Confederate history. County Galway-born Richard W. (Dick) Dowling was a first lieutenant commanding Company F, Texas Heavy Artillery. The unit is better known as the Davis Guards or the "Fighting Irishmen."

The Davis Guards comprised 45 enlisted men, one engineer, and one surgeon. All of the enlisted men were Irish, handpicked from the docks of Houston and Galveston and all in their twenties or younger.

In late 1863 Dowling and 42 of the Guards were dispatched by General Magruder to Fort Sabine, on the Gulf south of present-day Beaumont, to spike the six cannons there so they would be useless if captured, as well as to dismantle the fort. Instead of obeying orders, Dowling and his Irishmen proceeded to strengthen the earthen fort.

In September, 20 Federal ships carrying 5,000 men left New Orleans to invade Texas by way of Sabine Pass. They arrived off the Sabine bar on the night of the 7th. Three gunboats were given the task of putting the shore batteries out of action before landing the troops. Next morning they moved in on the silent and apparently deserted fort. One, the *Sachem*, made an attempt to gain the rear of the Confederate position. When they were within 1,200 yards, however, the

The Battle of Sabine Pass, September 5, 1863; Fort Sabine is on the peninsula (left).

silence was shattered by the roar of the six cannons. Devastating fire poured from the fort. For 45 minutes the Texas Irish furiously worked their guns, not even pausing to swab them. In that short time, they hurled 137 rounds at the enemy ships.

The *Sachem* was soon put out of action, and the Texas guns concentrated on the trailing *Clifton* and *Arizona*. The *Clifton* was disabled, and she and the *Sachem* surrendered. The *Arizona* prudently retired, and the Federal fleet sailed back to New Orleans.

Without the loss of a man, the 43 Confederate Irishmen had repulsed a Federal fleet, captured two gunboats, and taken 317 prisoners. Other Federal casualties were 19 killed, 9 wounded, and 37 missing. The Guards manned their fort for the remainder of the war.[4]

The Congress of the Confederate States passed a special resolution of thanks to the Davis Guards. The city of Houston raised $3,000 for them, and a proud state has remembered them and their courage in a monument at Sabine Pass bearing their names.

Dowling returned to Houston to reopen his saloon, called The Bank after the war, the Bank of Bacchus before. He is said to have organized the first oil company in Texas in 1866. He died in Houston and is buried in St. Vincent's Cemetery with many of the men who made history with him at Sabine Pass.

The Irish of San Antonio

The man sometimes known as San Antonio's "Breadline Banker" was Cork-born John Twohig, who, in 1830, established a mercantile business. He had taken part in the Siege of Béxar in December 1835 and was a city alderman at the time of Mexican General Adrian Woll's invasion of the city in 1842. He blew up his store so that the supplies and munitions would not fall into the hands of the invading Mexicans. Taken prisoner with 14 other San Antonians, he was lodged in Perote Prison, Mexico. Twohig and nine others escaped in July 1843, and Twohig returned to San Antonio. He opened a banking establishment in 1869 and became widely known for the personally financed breadline he maintained for the unfortunate of the city.[1] Twohig is buried in San Antonio's Old San Fernando Cemetery.

A contemporary of Twohig was Peter Gallagher, who was born in County Westmeath, Ireland, and, in 1837, came to San Antonio, where he worked as a stonemason. He was a member of the disastrous Santa Fe Expedition and kept, in his diary, a day-by-day account of the travels, capture, and imprisonment of the members of that group. After his release from the Mexican prison in 1842, he served as a Texas Ranger with the famous John C. Hays. He operated a mercantile business in San Antonio from 1846 to 1850, then returned to Ireland for his bride. When he came back to Texas, he developed business interests in San Antonio and Mexico and served as a justice of Bexar County. Gallagher started development of the Fort Stockton area and was instrumental in the organization of Pecos County.[2]

John Twohig and his residence on the San Antonio River

Among those who came to San Antonio in the late 1830's were three other Irish-born settlers who were to have some influence on the city's development. They were Bryan V. Callaghan, Edward Dwyer, and William Elliott.

Callaghan, a County Cork man, opened a store on Main Plaza. He married into the Ramón family and became influential in local politics, serving as mayor in 1845. If any man came close to establishing a political dynasty in the city of St. Anthony, that man would be Bryan V. Callaghan. His son, a lawyer, served first as city recorder and then nine terms as mayor. More than 100 years after Callaghan's coming to San Antonio, a descendant, Alfred Callaghan, was serving as mayor of the city.[3]

Edward Dwyer was a partner with William Elliott in a commercial business. In 1840 he served with José Antonio Navarro on a commission to investigate fraudulent land claims in the area. He, like Callaghan, married into one of the old San Antonio Spanish families. He served as mayor in 1845 and, at his death, owned extensive property in the city.[4]

William Elliott had served his apprenticeship in a mercantile house in Dublin, Ireland, and had come to America in 1820. In 1836 he was involved in mining in Mexico and had a merchandising business at Matamoros. In 1839, with Dwyer, he set up a San Antonio mercantile establishment.[5]

Two brothers who exemplify the tragedy of the Civil War had come to San Antonio about the mid-1840's. They were sons of William Devine of County

Portrait of Peter Gallagher by Edward Grenet

Judge Thomas J. Devine

Waterford, Ireland, who had fled to Nova Scotia because of involvement in the 1798 Uprising. Thomas J. Devine was an attorney, and his brother, James M., a doctor, and both became active in the political and civic life of the city. In the Civil War, they held opposing views.

Dr. James M. Devine served as treasurer of San Antonio (1848-1849) and was mayor for four terms between 1849 and 1857. As much committed to the Union cause as was his brother to that of the Confederacy, he left San Antonio on the outbreak of hostilities and went to live in Connecticut.

Thomas J. Devine served as city attorney from 1844 to 1850, when he became district attorney. In 1851 he was elected district judge of Bexar County and in 1861 was a member of the Secession Convention. He was one of the commission named to demand surrender of Federal troops and supplies in Texas. That same year he had joined the Confederate army but was named Confederate state judge for the Western District of Texas. During the war he also acted as emissary to Mexico to head off threatened troubles between that country and the Confederacy. After the war he was indicted for treason by the Federal government—one of only three so charged; the other two were Jefferson Davis and Clement Clay. In 1873 he was appointed a justice of the Texas Supreme Court and held that position until 1875, when he resigned to go into private practice. He served in 1881 as one of the regents of the then-planned University of Texas.[6]

Argyle Hotel, Alamo Heights, 1940. On St. Patrick's Day, 1893, Robert Emmit O'Grady and his sister, Alice O'Grady, opened their hotel in a former ranch house that had been converted into an inn by two Scotsmen. The O'Gradys enlarged the building and opened a dining room that became famous for its cuisine. Alice published her recipes in The Argyle Cookbook *in 1940, the year before her retirement.*

There was a large influx of Irish settlers to San Antonio in the 1840's. A number were reported living in an area known as the "Irish Flats" in 1842. During the war with Mexico, many Irish-born came to Texas with the United States Army and later settled in San Antonio. The Irish continued to come to San Antonio, as to other areas of Texas, in the years following. Some were associated with the military, either as army personnel or in civilian capacities, and others were artisans, merchants, and politicians. Among the families who settled in San Antonio in the 19th century were the Duffys, Tynans, Collinses, Dillons, Buckleys, McDermotts, Morans, Shannons, Dolans, Downeys, Stevenses, Cosgroves, and many others. They were so numerous that a complete listing would appear as a roll call of the Celtic clans, and they gave substance to the contention that, without the support of the Irish, no man could be elected to public office in the city of San Antonio.

The houses of Irish Flats were constructed mostly of soft stone quarried on the outskirts of the city. The residents all built and owned their homes. The building of a house for a newcomer was usually an occasion in which all the

George Henry Noonan, whose parents came from Limerick, became a resident of Castroville, then of San Antonio. In 1862 he was elected judge of the Eighteenth Judicial District of Texas. Elected in succeeding terms, he served as district judge until 1894, when he resigned to become a United States congressman. Noonan was also known as a prominent rancher who owned one of the largest horse ranches in the Southwest.

neighbors volunteered their services. Such cooperative effort was also the occasion for celebration.

Life in the Irish community reflected the gaiety and generosity of the Irish spirit. The "latch string" was always out, and no one ever went hungry or lacked a friend. Ebullient Celtic spirits found outlet in the weekly Saturday-night dances at which, in a continuation of the old Irish custom, anyone having a special talent was called on for a demonstration of Irish step-dancing, a musical piece, a song, or an oratorical presentation. Those present might be entertained by an Irish reel, with fiddle or accordion leading flying feet through the intricate steps. Again, renditions like "Emmet's Speech from the Dock" would recall remnants of Irish history. Thus, in the manner of the ancient *filidh* (learned ones) were preserved the music, history, and lore of the green fields and mist-shrouded hills that were so far from the sun-baked adobe and dusty plazas of a southwestern Texas town.

They mourned their dead in the traditional way of the Celt—a grieving for the lost one which was also a rejoicing for the soul that, through death, was freed of the trials of life. Refreshments were served, and tobacco-filled clay pipes, coffee, whiskey, and beer (when that beverage came in later in the century) were offered to those attending the "wake."

They enjoyed life, but, in the words of one Irishman, "never forgot Him Whose gift it was and to Whom it must be returned." The Irish were numerous enough and devoted enough to join other English-speaking Catholics to form a parish and build the beautiful St. Mary's Catholic Church.[7]

The very business expansion and city growth to which the Irish contributed brought changes to the Irish Flats. Imperceptible at first, the movement out of the Flats gained momentum with the passing years as residents moved to areas where they or their fathers had, in earlier times, clashed with Indians. Some of the descendants of the old Irish melted into the general American community with nothing to distinguish them except a surname. Others, clinging to the ancient heritage, moved toward a new Irish community that, with the building of Fort Sam Houston, was developing adjacent to that post. The new community centered on St. Patrick's Catholic Church—built on the city's northeast side to accommodate the later generations of San Antonio Irish.

The Irish of the Corpus Christi Area

The development of Corpus Christi was due, in no small part, to the Irish of San Patricio and the Irish who came in the 1840's, 1850's, and 1860's. In 1844 there were only three women living in the town—Mrs. Mary Heffernan Riggs, a German lady, and a Mexican lady. Mrs. Riggs's father had, with his cousin, brother, and brother's family, been massacred by Indians in 1835.

In 1845 the then-unincorporated town became the port of entry for General Zachary Taylor's United States Army on its way to the Rio Grande and the Mexican War. His army contained many Irish-born Americans who, becoming acquainted with the Texas Irish, returned to settle in the area when the war with Mexico was over. Among those was a Matthew Dunn, who wrote to his relatives in Ireland extolling the beauty and potential of Texas. His brothers, Peter and Thomas, and their families came to Corpus Christi in 1850. They were joined by brother John in 1851 and by Patrick in 1868.[1]

Other Irish settled in the young town for different reasons. In the early 1850's, an Irish sea captain, James McBride, put into port at Corpus Christi. There he met Mary Dunn, daughter of Peter. They were soon married, and McBride exchanged his seafaring life for that of a Texas rancher.

Nueces County had been created in 1846, and Richard Powers was one of the first county commissioners. H.N. Barry was elected sheriff, and Edward Fitzgerald, county clerk. In the late 1840's, Charles Callihan was editor of the local newspaper, the *Corpus Christi Star*.[2]

Former Irish sea captain James McBride (center) with his wife and children

An agent of Henry L. Kinney, founder of Corpus Christi, had canvassed Ireland in the late 1840's for people to settle the area. He advertised the advantages of the site as a trading post. So many people responded that, in 1852, Kinney established a settlement called Nuecestown with people largely from Ireland. It was some miles from Corpus Christi on the Nueces River.

Corpus Christi had a strong Irish concentration in an area known as "Irishtown." This developed into a 27-block area bounded by present-day Twigg Street, Mesquite Street, Brewster Street, and the bay. Here, in imposing one- and two-story houses, resided lawyers, judges, doctors, merchants, farmers, and cattlemen. The area had its own fire-fighting unit known as the Shamrock Hose Company. It also had a baseball team, which maintained a friendly rivalry with that of "Dutchtown," located along the beach to the south.

The first resident Catholic priest in Corpus Christi (1853) was Dublin-born Father Bernard O'Reilly, and the first Catholic Church was St. Patrick's, finished in 1857. Prior to Father O'Reilly's pastorate, the area had been served by the pastor from Victoria—County Mayo-born Father James Fitzgerald.[3]

St. Patrick's Church in Corpus Christi

> Among the Irish founding families of old St. Patrick's were those of Martin Kelly; Joseph FitzSimmons; James Ranahan; Richard Gallagher; John, Peter, and Matthew Dunn; Cornelius Cahill; Richard Powers; Dr. John Cleary; Patrick O'Docherty; James McBride; James Feely; and Dennis Whelan.[4]

A Texas university owes its existence in part to Father O'Reilly's interest in the establishment of a school for boys. In his will he bequeathed his Corpus Christi property for that purpose, so the proceeds were used for the building of a boys' school near Dallas. Today that school is the University of Dallas. Father O'Reilly had hoped the school would be in Corpus Christi, but the Vincentian Fathers of St. Louis, to whom he had left the property, decided otherwise.[5]

Political activity is second nature to the Irish. Corpus Christi provides evidence of the power of the Irish vote in the early days. From 1854, two years after the city was incorporated, until 1886, Irish-named individuals served as selected city officials in every year except 1855. Under the Texas Constitution of 1876 and from that year until 1900, 18 of the 52 county commissioners were Irish. During the same 25-year period, Joseph FitzSimmons served as county judge for 16 years.[6]

Father Bernard O'Reilly   *Cornelius Cahill*

Irishtown home of Charlotte Gallagher Hutchinson, Corpus Christi

Cornelius Cahill and his wife were natives of County Kerry, Ireland. They had migrated to New York, then to Texas in the early 1850's. Cahill served as alderman of Corpus Christi in 1854 and later as a county judge. Among Mrs. Cahill's most treasured possessions were a crucifix, shawl, and seashells, all brought from Kerry. Since even today Gaelic is spoken in that part of Ireland, it is not surprising that the Cahills were fluent in the language. It is recorded that Mrs. Cahill taught her black servant girl "to say her prayers in the Irish language." A daughter, Johanna, was one of Corpus Christi's first schoolteachers and commuted daily on horseback to the country school where she taught.[7]

Among the Irish who responded to Colonel Kinney's promotion of Corpus Christi was Richard Gallagher and his family. A sheep farmer of County Westmeath, Gallagher sold his flock in Ireland and, in 1852, set sail with his family for Texas on the *Star of the West*. He bought a tract of land on Oso Creek, west of Corpus Christi, and went into sheep raising. Land then was cheap and plentiful in that part of the country—as low as 50 cents per acre—and there was no conflict between cattlemen and sheep raisers.

The Gallaghers prospered. Corpus Christi was developing as a port and, between 1870 and 1880, was considered the nation's largest wool-handling port. However, in the 1880's, a deadly disease afflicted sheep in the region, and the Gallaghers turned to cattle raising on their Oso Ranch. Later they went into dealing in grain and cotton.

Richard Gallagher died in 1881, leaving a daughter and two sons. One son, John, later moved into Corpus Christi. He became the principal stockholder of the State National Bank and served as county commissioner and as city councilman, and his income from those public offices was donated to charity.[8]

Today's descendants of those pioneer Irish Texans maintain a strong sense of identity with their past in the treasured mementos, the repeated anecdotes, and the remembered, but not always understood, terms.

Corpus Christi residents Mrs. Rachel Hébert and Mrs. Irene Peters had, for years, puzzled over the term "sally rod." When, as a child learning needlework, Mrs. Peters would use a needle that was too long for the task at hand, her Irish-born aunt would tell her to use the correct needle instead of "that sally rod." It was only on a trip to the west of Ireland that Mrs. Hébert discovered that the "sally" is a form of willow. Because of its strength and flexibility, the shoots, or rods, are used to pin down the straw of thatched roofs.

Cherished items include a four-poster bed brought by the Gallaghers from Ireland, a pair of mittens knitted by an Irish forebear, and a Union cannonball. The ball was fired by a Federal warship during the Civil War siege of Corpus Christi and passed through the Irishtown shellcrete house of Mrs. Charlotte Kelly, sister to Mrs. Richard Gallagher. A descendant of the Cahill family treasures a pair of spurs worn by a member of that family at the time he was shot by an assassin.[9]

The all-night wakes for the dead are still remembered, and any mention of that brings to mind the incident of "Auntie Kelly's shroud."

Many in Ireland belonged to the nonmonastic laymen's group of the Franciscans known as "the Third Order." Except for special religious occasions, the brown-cowled habit, or robe, was not worn but was carefully put away so that, at death, it might be placed on the member's body as a shroud. Emigrating Irish members of the Third Order brought such robes with them. Auntie Kelly, a member of the Gallagher family, had such a robe carefully packed away against the time it would be needed. The bureau drawer in which it was stored was "off limits" to her three nieces, who liked to visit her.

To the children the forbidden robe was a shroud with a capital *S*, and, with the morbid interest that adds delicious terror to childish curiosity, "that bureau drawer was to be investigated at the first opportunity." The opportunity came one day when the aunt was absent from the house. There was a rush for the bureau. The most daring pulled the drawer out slowly and, to the "ohs" and "ahs" of the other conspirators, drew out and unfolded the forbidden robe.

Familiarity invites further familiarity, and before long each was taking a turn trying on the cowled garment. But "what good was a shroud without a wake?" A noisy argument settled the question of who would be "waked." The "deceased," occupying the upper half of the robe, stretched out on the floor between two unlit candles. The hands were properly clasped, eyes closed, and features frozen into immobility. On either side the wails of the two "mourners" were punctuated by compliments—one never spoke ill of the dead at an Irish wake. Suddenly, in what seemed a "call to judgment," the "dead" heard her name uttered in a loud, shocked voice. Auntie Kelly had returned. The three miscreants leapt to their feet and contritely waited for an unplanned sequel to their little drama—the "temporal punishment" due to sin.

Fortunately, Auntie Kelly was a very understanding adult, who, afterwards, laughed as heartily as anyone at the mischievous escapade of her nieces.[10]

Another story regarding a "Third Order robe" was told to John W. Meaney of Austin by his maternal grandfather, John Dunn Jr. of Corpus Christi. In 1867 a dreadful yellow fever epidemic had hit Corpus Christi and the surrounding countryside, carrying off many settlers. In August five members of the Dunn family living on the ranch west of Corpus Christi died from it. John Dunn Jr. was 14 years old when his mother contracted the disease and was confined to her bed. The boy always believed she would recover. This hardy Irishwoman had survived a three-month voyage from Ireland, had helped her husband meet the challenges of the frontier, and had provided a home that was a haven of warmth and security for the nine children. She would not die. Anne Dunn summoned him to her bedside. She smiled regretfully at him and laid a wasted, fever-hot hand on his. "John," she said, "bring me the Third Order robe from Whelan's"—and as he hesitated, not wanting to believe the import of the

Professor Robert Francis Dougherty

request—"quick now!" Fighting back the tears, he left the room and, mounting his saddle pony, rode with a heavy heart the two or three miles to the Whelan place. When he returned with the robe, his mother was already dead.[11]

Corpus Christi descendants of the Doughertys of San Patricio recall with pride the part played in local education by grandfather Robert Dougherty. Prior to 1868 this highly educated County Donegal man had taught school at San Patricio, where he had settled. From 1868 to 1874, he taught at Hidalgo Seminary in Corpus Christi. Afterwards he returned as a teacher to San Patricio, where, in 1876, he established a boys' boarding school. The two-story building, in an excellent state of preservation, stands near the McGloin house at Round Lake just west of San Patricio.

Teaching provided little monetary compensation in those days, and Dougherty had to find time to work his land and tend his livestock. However, even then, his books were never far away. In 1866 Robert Dougherty was in the area of San Diego, Duval County, gathering horses that belonged to him and his brother, James, who was killed in the Civil War. From there he wrote the following letter to his wife at San Patricio:

San Diego, August 15, 1866

My dear Rachel,

Another opportunity to send you a few lines is afforded. The bearer Captain McGuire, an Irishman and apparently a gentleman of intelligence, reached here a few days ago from Mexico. He says he is a cousin of Martin O'Toole and Mrs. Corrigan, is about two years from the old country, has been a captain in the British Army in India which position he resigned to join Finians. He was on his way to San Antonio in company of Fisher the adjutant of Hank's regiment and another gentleman; but finding out that the O'Toole family lived near San Patricio, he changes his course and goes by the Aransas. Treat him politely and kindly for he has all the appearances and manner of a well-bred Irishman.

McCowan will return with a wagon to this place. If he can he will take the little things that are there. If your mother has two boxes of candles I wish to get one. I thought I would not need any so soon, so I did not buy any in Corpus. Pistol caps and powder will sell here too. Write me by McCowan. My things have not yet come. Did Hank and your mother yet go to Corpus? Send me my shoes. George and John James have gone to Junction 15 miles from this place today. This Fiesta begins tomorrow. They will be going home in three or four days. I shall have another chance to write by them. Be sure of sending writing paper.

I remain, my dearest Rachel,
Your affectionate husband
R. Dougherty

My regards to all, and send Cooper's Virgil.[12]

The letter and postscript indicate that the "raw and savage" frontier was not thoroughly so, that mingling with gunmen and hired "bravos" were men of sensitivity and learning who could be concerned about the reception given a "well-bred" visitor and look forward to the companionship of a book.

There persists in Corpus Christi a story that Peter Dunn and his family crossed the Atlantic in "a sailboat," but details are hard to pin down. Since most oceangoing vessels of that day were sail-rigged, and since, even today, only mariners make the distinction between "ship" and "boat," the story is true. However, it also appears to be an example of Irish imagination and Texas tongue-in-cheek storytelling.

As told by J. Patrick Dunne of Corpus Christi, those "sailboats"—there was more than one—were responsible for quite a bit more than just transporting the Dunn(e)s to Texas. "In the beginning," recounted Pat with a solemnity that belied the twinkle in his eye, "our name in Ireland was Dynne, and two Dynne families, each in its own sailboat, left County Sligo for Texas at the same time the O'Loughlin family was setting out in its craft. Through mishandling, the

Robert Dougherty's residence, Round Lake, near San Patricio, 1979. Completed in 1876, the structure originally housed St. Paul's Academy and living quarters for the Dougherty family.

O'Loughlin boat and one Dynne boat sideswiped. The *O* was stripped off the O'Loughlin boat, and the final *e* and bottom part of the *y* was stripped from the Dynne boat. That branch of the family is since known as 'Dunn.' My family's boat led the flotilla and plowed so fast through the waves that the bottom part of the *y* was worn off. Ever since, we spell our name Dunne."

A key to the origin of the above story and a no-nonsense account of life in the Corpus Christi area through three generations is contained in two unpublished accounts by members of the Dunn family. They refer to John Dunn and family setting out for Texas "in a small sailing vessel" and taking 11 weeks for the voyage from Liverpool. The accounts are of triumphs and tragedies—of five members of the family succumbing, within five days, to a yellow fever epidemic and of two Dunns treacherously shot to death. In 1864 Confederate soldier Lawrence Dunn, home on furlough, was shot from ambush by a member of a gang of cattle thieves with which he was parleying under a white flag. In 1868 Matt Dunn was shot in the back by members of a group of Mexicans which he had befriended.[13]

As proof that music can "soothe the savage breast," Irish melodies wafting over the southwest prairie calmed the anger of a would-be lynching party that dogged the steps of a small posse and its prisoners. An account is given of Mike and John Dunn Jr., members of the Texas Rangers at that time, and others apprehending, in 1874, some self-confessed killers near the Penescal Ranch. Four men had been killed on the ranch, and an angry mob had threatened lynch law. As the Dunns and the deputy sheriff started back to Corpus Christi, some 60 miles away, with their prisoners, there were ominous rumblings that they would never get through the *brasada* (brush country). "But the deputy sheriff was a very good singer and he immediately began loudly singing old Irish songs which he kept up most of the way to Corpus Christi. The mob's spirit was already on the wane; this sound of Irish singing in the ears of San Patricio County may have been just the thing that finally overthrew them."[14]

John B. Dunn (left) and his son John, 1890's. John B. Dunn was a packinghouse worker, trailhand, rancher, businessman, and Texas Ranger. He recorded many of his adventures in The Perilous Trails of Texas. *A collector of military artifacts and other memorabilia, Dunn opened a museum for his collection in Corpus Christi. "Red John," as he was called, was the son of Matthew Dunn and a nephew of John Dunn Sr.*

The Liberty-Beaumont Areas

The Liberty and Jefferson County areas lay within the general boundaries of an empresario grant made by the Mexican government in the late 1820's to a group headed by Joseph Vehlein. Vehlein turned over the work of colonization to a real estate promotion firm, the Galveston Bay and Texas Land Company; however, Mexico refused to recognize the company's land assignments. Since this part of Texas was just west of the Sabine River, across from Louisiana, it presented an alluring enticement to would-be settlers from the southern United States. Perhaps not knowing, or not caring, whether the titles to their acquisitions were recognized, many came to occupy the land, including a number of Americans of Irish descent.

Even before the land was opened for settlement, the family of James McFaddin had come to Texas by way of Louisiana. They, with others, arrived in 1822 in Atascosita, a small town on the Trinity River, and took up land in the region, forming the settlement which later became Liberty. By 1833 the McFaddins were living on property that would be taken in by the town of Beaumont.

In 1832 angry colonists marched upon the Mexican garrison at Anahuac on Galveston Bay, in part because the Mexican commander refused to recognize the municipality and *ayuntamiento* (town council) of Liberty. Thus, it is not surprising that, in 1835, the town contributed its own military unit, the Liberty Volunteers, to the Texas cause. Among the Irish-named members of the unit

Spindletop Oil Field, near Beaumont, 1900's

which successfully regained San Antonio at the Siege of Béxar, was James McFaddin's 16-year-old son, William M. In March 1836 William again volunteered, with Liberty's 3rd Infantry, 2nd Regiment, under the command of Captain W.H. Logan, and joined General Houston in the Battle of San Jacinto, where he was assigned with other boy-soldiers to guard the Texas baggage train.

One of William's sons, W.P.H. "Perry" McFaddin, went into the cattle business with his father in 1877. An innovator, he experimented with the commercial raising of muskrats and initiated the milling of rice in Beaumont, giving the city a new enterprise.[1]

Another influential citizen of the Beaumont area, George Washington O'Brien had, in 1849 at age 16, left the home of his half brother in Louisiana and made his way to Texas to join his father, also named George, son of Irish immigrant Christopher Bryan (O'Brien).

Christopher had left Dublin in the last half of the 18th century, having stowed away on a ship bound for America after the king's guard saw him poaching deer. He had fought in the American Revolutionary War, then spent some years with his family in Kentucky. Several of his children moved on to Louisiana and

George Washington O'Brien

prospered in indigo and corn; one of them, George W.'s father, went to Texas after his wife died in 1833. Before he died, Christopher Bryan told his family that his name had been O'Brien in Ireland, but he had changed it to Bryan to help hide his identity, and he wanted his family to henceforth use "O'Brien."

In 1852 George Washington O'Brien became mail rider for the Galveston to Beaumont beach route, and it was in Beaumont that he married and became active in community affairs, serving as county clerk and justice of the peace. In 1861 he received his license to practice law.

Although he spoke against secession at the county convention in 1861, O'Brien nevertheless joined his neighbors to help form Company F, Fifth Texas Infantry Regiment, better known as Hood's Texas Brigade. Stricken with a severe case of measles while on duty in Virginia, he was discharged for disability and recuperation and hiked on foot back to Texas. By the time he arrived there, his health had so improved that he reported immediately to the Texas Confederate command. Impressed by his loyalty to the cause, the Confederate staff commissioned him to return to Beaumont to recruit a company and to serve as its captain.

O'Brien remained in Beaumont after the war. Late in 1865 he received a letter from a fellow soldier asking him to buy up all the land he could around Spindletop Hill for the purpose of reselling it to oil speculators, for oil had been discovered in Pennsylvania in 1859. Remembering how his troops had amused themselves while they were camped there by lighting the gas that escaped, and recalling the oily substance that oozed from the ground nearby, O'Brien must have read the letter with great interest.

In 1866 he was privy to some conversations with oil prospector B.T. Kavanaugh, who used a divining rod to determine trace veins of coal, oil, and other subterranean substances. O'Brien was able to secure part of the Spindletop property in 1888, and when Patillo Higgins and George Washington Carroll secured the rest of it in 1892 with the intention of operating a brick factory using the convenient fuel, negotiations were in order. The Gladys City Oil, Gas and Manufacturing Company was incorporated in 1892 with the controlling interest owned by the O'Brien family, George and his widowed daughter, Emma E. John. Drilling began in 1893, but the big strike at Spindletop, the Lucas Gusher, arrived on January 10, 1901, appropriately ushering in a new century and a new industry for Texas.[2]

From 1836 to 1900, Irish contributions to the commercial and political development of the Liberty-Beaumont area are indicated by the names that appear: Dr. Henry Foley, who was practicing medicine in Liberty in 1836 and was mayor in 1838; Christopher Bryan, who came to Liberty in 1840 and in 1855 was postmaster and operated the City Hotel; Martha Fitzgerald, operator in 1860 of the Traveler's Hotel; R.E. Kelly, who in 1889 established Beaumont's *Journal*, a weekly newspaper which became a daily in 1898; and A.J. McCormick, who was mayor of Liberty from 1884 to 1889 and from 1892 to 1894. The crews of the shallow-draft steamboats that plied the Trinity River between Dallas and the Gulf often heard orders given in the rich Irish brogue. Some 20 captains and pilots of such vessels in the 40-year period 1838-1878 carried Irish names ranging from Burke to Sweeney.[3]

Irish Railroaders and Houston-Galveston

The first length of Texas railroad was put into operation in 1853. It was a 25-mile track connecting Harrisburg and Brazoria.[1] By 1870 Texas had 711 miles of track and by 1888, 8,211 miles.[2] Irish labor and Irish entrepreneurship contributed to this expansion. Irish were to be found in the executive offices of the railroad companies as well as in the labor gangs.

As laborers they worked for $2 per day as ironmen laying rail, headspikers, fish-plate bolters, track liners, and back-ironmen. They developed a rhythm in the work, to which they sang such songs as "Pat Malloy," "Brinon on the Moor," "Poor Paddy He Works on the Railroad," and "Drill, Ye Tarriers, Drill." [3] Occasionally, they had to contest the Indians for the prairie, but, since so many were veterans of the Union and Confederate armies, the use of the rifle was second nature to them. The minimum goal was a mile of track a day, whether under a broiling sun or in the icy blast of a prairie winter. At day's end, far from towns and following the road they made, they slept in the three-tiered bunks of a rail car bunkhouse. Sunday was a day of rest, and, in the absence of priests, the mostly Catholic Irish laborers would retire in small groups to pray their beads. Many, having accumulated a small stake, would eventually take up land near a terminal. Thus were the Irish of the post-Civil War period scattered across the state along the railroad lines. Many of the early Irish Texan pioneers had given their names to towns associated with their businesses or ranches: Callahan in Webb County, Port Sullivan in Milam, Sullivan City in Hidalgo, Hearne in Robertson, McMahan in Caldwell, Bryan in Brazos, and Monahans in Ward. In addition, Irish railroaders' names were given to railroad stations or junctures that later grew into towns. Higgins in Lipscomb County was named for G.H. Higgins, a prominent stockholder of the Panhandle and Santa Fe Railroad; Killeen in Bell for Frank P. Killeen, official of the Gulf, Colorado, and Santa Fe; Carey in Childress for an employee of the Fort Worth and Denver; O'Brien in Haskell for a superintendent of the Kansas City, Mexico, and Orient; and Moran in Shackelford for John J. Moran, president of the Missouri, Kansas, and Texas. There are between 40 and 50 such towns.[4]

There are Texas counties named after Irishmen, but it is the small towns, ranches, and farms throughout the state connected with them that constitute the real barometer of Irish penetration of the wilderness and of the Irish industry that contributed to Texas's development.

Many Irish who had served at San Jacinto moved to Galveston after the war. Later arrivals of the 19th century apparently sensed the potential of the Houston-Galveston area. They flocked there from the Irish counties of Mayo, Galway, Kerry, Cork, Sligo, Leitrim, Cayan, Queens, Westmeath, Tipperary, Dublin, and Down. The development of those two cities as centers of trade and commerce is closely bound up with the activities of Irish businessmen and railroaders. From 1836 to the 1860's, Galveston had dominated the area as a port of entry for ocean trade. An existing railroad system moved freight from the port through Houston. However, among the Houston promoters were Irishmen who envisioned that city as a deep-water port and trade terminal to exceed Galveston.

Following the Civil War, John Thomas Brady organized the Texas Transportation Company to build a railroad and the New Houston City Company to develop a proposed juncture of rail and water transport facilities. John Shearn's Houston Direct Navigation Company of 1869 set about developing port facilities, while his Buffalo Bayou Ship Channel Company worked on improving the channel. Houston Mayor Thomas H. Scanlan used the powers of his office to further the projects to develop port facilities. In 1889 Brady chartered the Houston Belt and Magnolia Park Railway Company to connect all the transportation lines, which would, it was hoped, entice oceangoing vessels to bring their cargoes to Houston. Meanwhile, aid was given two small railroad lines to extend their tracks from Houston to the interior of the state.[5]

Because of these efforts, the Galveston trade declined, and much was transferred to Houston. The Galveston 1867 yellow fever epidemic also hurt the ocean port. During the epidemic an embargo—as much political as medical—was placed by Houston on goods coming from Galveston. So much trade was rerouted directly to Houston at the time, that the embargo was reinstated each time there was the least hint of a Galveston yellow fever outbreak.[6]

Something had to be done in Galveston. In 1873 the city obtained a charter for the Gulf, Colorado, and Santa Fe Railway. Among the prime movers were

Loading cotton, Buffalo Bayou Ship Channel, Houston, c. 1900; Houston and Texas Central Railroad in background.

W.L. Moody and George Sealy. Sealy was one of 10 children of an Irish family from Pennsylvania. He had worked for a Pennsylvania railroad and, at age 22, had joined a cotton brokerage firm. Although opposing slavery, he joined the Confederate army, where he served without pay. After the war he moved to Galveston and made a small fortune in cotton and banking. He had invested $250,000 in the Gulf, Colorado, and Santa Fe railroad, but, at the end of three years, it had built only 60 miles of track.

When, in 1879, the railroad was offered for sale, Sealy bought it and set about revitalizing the company. By 1885 the company had a rail system from Galveston and Houston to Dallas, Fort Worth, and Lampasas. At that time the New York financier, Jay Gould, had established a stranglehold on Texas commerce trying to reach northern markets through control of the lines entering the state from the north and east. George Sealy drove his line north and across Oklahoma Indian Territory to connect with the Atchison, Topeka, and Santa Fe. Gould's grip on Texas commerce was broken, and Texas goods could now reach northern markets.[7]

Nicholas J. Clayton, architect in Galveston from 1872 until his death in 1916. Born in Cork in 1849, he studied architecture, structural engineering, and sculpture. Clayton received architectural commissions throughout Texas. Among the most notable works in Galveston are the Bishop's Palace and the Medical Department of the University of Texas (below).

Prior to the battles of the industrial and railroad giants, the foundations for Galveston's development had been laid. Among the builders of those foundations were Irishmen. Christopher Fox, born in Ireland in 1811, came to Texas in 1837. He was a baker by trade and was active in Galveston civic affairs. Apparently he was a man of strong convictions. He stood for the Union, and, when Texas seceded, he closed his business and did not reopen it until after the cessation of hostilities.[8]

Irish-born Charles R. Hughes came to Texas in the late 1830's, bringing much-needed accounting skills to the fledgling republic. He became associated with William Hennelly and Company and in 1858 established his own commission house. Hughes was active in the city's civic, social, and religious life.[9]

The Protestant Episcopal Church of Texas owes its formal beginnings to 36-year-old Dublin-born Reverend Benjamin Eaton, who arrived in Galveston on January 14, 1841. He held the first service in private rooms but, realizing the limitations of such arrangements, was determined to build a church. He went to the United States to raise money for this purpose, and on June 26, 1842, the first Episcopal Church in Texas opened for services in Galveston.[10]

Irish-born M. Quin had come to Texas in 1856 to work with the Harrisburg and San Antonio Railway. When the Civil War broke out, he joined the Confederate army and served throughout the war with Company H, 16th Texas Infantry. In 1867 he entered the cotton brokerage business and later organized an insurance company. He was elected to the state legislature in 1876.[11]

P.H. Hennessey, County Limerick-born and a brother-in-law of Dick Dowling, came to America in 1849 and to Texas in 1851. He served with the Confederacy throughout the Civil War as a lieutenant of the Davis Guards. A successful businessman active in local affairs, he served on the city council and as school director of Galveston County.[12]

William Boyd was born in Ireland in 1840. At 16 he came to New Orleans, where he learned the cotton business. He entered Confederate service and was promoted to captain. After the war he engaged in steamboating and came to Galveston in 1871. Boyd entered the cotton business in that city and served as a member of the city council.[13]

All of God's Children

Volumes would be required to render a complete account of Irish contributions to Texas in the fields of religion, education, social work, and medical care. However, for a contribution that is distinctively Texan and Irish, the efforts of a Kerry-born Irishwoman are unique. Her work resulted in the first Texas religious foundation for women.[1]

As a child in Ireland, Margaret Mary Healy had seen the sufferings of her people—outcasts in their own land denied education, property, and political rights. Her mother, Jane Murphy Healy, died when she was five. In 1845 her doctor father, his health broken in service to his impoverished neighbors, left his youngest daughter with relatives and, with his older children and other relatives, joined the emigrants seeking a better life in the New World. They came to a farm in Virginia. Here Margaret Mary saw the extremes of wealth and poverty, discrimination and prejudice arising through ignorance and lack of formal education. She and her two aunts volunteered as lay teachers in a nonsectarian Sunday school established by local Irish and German settlers.

The family decided to move to Texas, but her father died in New Orleans en route. She and her two brothers accompanied her two uncles and aunts to Matamoros, Mexico, from which city they hoped to enter Texas. While there, they opened a hotel. From Matamoros her brothers and one uncle left for the California gold fields. Margaret Mary Healy spent the years 1846 to 1850 with her aunts in Matamoros. The hotel prospered, although the Mexican frontier town was not peaceful. Desperadoes often robbed and killed with seeming impunity. The young Irish girl saw her uncle, John Murphy, gunned down on the porch of their home by a fleeing bandit.

The mid-1840's were also the years of the Mexican War, and among the Irish volunteers in General Zachary Taylor's army was Cork-born John B. Murphy. Following his service in the army, he remained in the Southwest and, in 1848, opened a commercial business in Matamoros, where he met Margaret Mary Healy. They were married on her 16th birthday, May 4, 1849.

The Murphys moved to Texas in 1850. John had started a law practice in Corpus Christi, and, in that year, he brought his young bride to a 4,000-acre ranch he had purchased in the San Patricio area. The lawlessness that characterized the Nueces River area did not abate with Texas's admission to the Union. Freebooters still roamed, destroying homes, driving off livestock, and generally terrorizing the habitants. With a reputation as an excellent horsewoman always possessed of a good mount, Mrs. Murphy was unconcerned for her own safety. She brought material aid and consolation to the victims of local violence. Conditions worsened with the outbreak of the Civil War, and she opened a small clinic and soup kitchen at her home. Many of the people, unable to endure the constant pillage and harassment, eventually moved from the San Patricio area. The Murphy ranch was also plundered during this time, and, in 1846, the Murphys moved into Corpus Christi, where they lived in a home at Water and William streets.

The 1867 yellow fever epidemic hit Corpus Christi particularly hard, carrying off whole families. Mrs. Murphy continued her ministrations. During this time she saw many of her friends and fellow workers die from the disease, but this did not deter her.

The effects of the Civil War were felt for many years in Corpus Christi. It had become economically impoverished, and "education was almost frozen." The lack of public schools meant that children roamed the streets. Education was also seen as the basic need of the recently freed blacks if they were to overcome their handicaps. Mrs. Murphy wrote to Bishop Dubuis, outlining the problems and requesting that nuns be obtained to tend to the education of the young.

At the request of the Texas bishop, the Sisters of Mary in Belgium sent three nuns to Waco, Texas, in 1873. One of them was Sister Angela, formerly Jane Healy, blood sister to Mrs. Murphy. Unknown to the latter, her sister Jane had been sent to France for her education. She later entered the Order of the Sisters of Mary and was assigned to Texas.

A hurricane in 1875 left many in Corpus Christi homeless. Mrs. Murphy constituted a one-woman relief agency, distributing necessary food and clothing. She purchased some property on Antelope Street and converted the three buildings on it into temporary shelters for the homeless. The unpretentious buildings became known as "Mrs. Murphy's hospital for the poor." Everyone in

Margaret Mary Healy Murphy *Judge John B. Murphy*

need was welcome: Anglo-Americans, Mexican Americans, African Americans, with no differentiation made.

John B. Murphy had established a good law practice and was active in the civic and political affairs of Corpus Christi. He served as a delegate from Nueces County to the Constitutional Convention in 1875 and was appointed to a number of state committees. He was later appointed as a state district judge, then, in 1880, he became mayor of Corpus Christi. Worn down by his work, Judge Murphy died in July 1884.

Margaret Mary Murphy was now alone. She and her husband had had no children, and the two girls they had adopted had entered religious service. Her younger aunt, Johanna Murphy, died on July 11, 1884, and her surviving aunt, Mary Murphy, had married James McGloin of San Patricio. When invited to Temple, Texas, to teach the blacks in that town, Mrs. Murphy went with two companions, but the effort failed. After returning from Temple, she visited San Antonio, which had a large and growing black population.

There were no formal schools for blacks in San Antonio, and countless children roamed the streets. In 1887 Mrs. Murphy rented accommodations near St. Joseph's Church on Commerce Street. She sold off a portion of the San Patricio

Sisters of the Holy Ghost and their students at St. Peter Claver Church, San Antonio

ranch, purchased property at Nolan and Live Oak streets with the proceeds, and had a church, a convent, and school facilities built on the site. The building contractor was E.J. Gallagher.

The property was in an exclusively white neighborhood, and there was opposition to the project. Work on the buildings was stopped twice—first, on the objections of residents in the area, and, when that failed, on complaints through city authorities about materials used in construction. The latter also was overridden, and the substantial buildings are still in use today.

Opposition did not cease with completion of the buildings. Stories are told of stones hurtling through the windows and of people who had volunteered to help in the school being snubbed by old friends. Those who might have helped the institution were loudest in their opposition to it.

The school opened in 1888. The enrollment consisted of day students and boarding students, and none were turned away. As enrollment grew, so did Mrs. Murphy's problems. Prejudice produced an incessant clamor of opposition to the school, and new problems arose from a shortage of dedicated teachers. Finally, on the suggestion of her sister, who was now superior of the Sacred Heart Academy at Waco, and the advice of Bishop Neraz, she decided to form

Mother Margaret Mary Healy Murphy

her own congregation of sisters to care for the school. Three of the teachers formed with her, on June 6, 1892, the nucleus of a religious community to be known afterwards as the Sisters of the Holy Ghost. As superior and founder, she was known as Mother Margaret Mary Healy Murphy. The Sisters of the Holy Ghost was the first religious order founded in Texas.

Mother Margaret Mary was asked to open a similar school in Victoria; later, schools were opened in Laredo and in Mexico, and there was a need for more sisters. In 1896 and again in 1899, Mother Margaret Mary visited Ireland to recruit candidates for the order. She returned with 12 postulants, and, in later years, self-sacrificing Irishwomen continued to swell the ranks of the Sisters of the Holy Ghost so that, today, about 90 percent of the membership is Irish-born.

This remarkable woman died on August 25, 1907. With the passage of civil rights legislation and the elimination of segregation in public education, some of the problems that faced Mother Margaret Mary no longer exist. However, her order has applied itself to the problems of a society far removed from the one she knew in the 19th century.[2] Today, Sisters of the Holy Spirit work out of some 39 missions in Texas, Louisiana, and Mississippi. They conduct a home for the aged in Brownsville. The location on Nolan Street in San Antonio, where Mother Margaret Mary started her first school, is now the Healy-Murphy Center. Here they educate school dropouts, those who cannot function in a regular school situation. The multifaceted program is no longer limited to blacks, and the institution has become nondenominational.

Honorable Mention

A complete and detailed recording of the contributions of all the Irish settlers in Texas exceeds the limitations of this short work. The following are a few noteworthy examples:

Dr. Alexander W. Ewing (1809-1853) was born in Derry (Londonderry), Ireland. He studied medicine at Trinity College, Dublin, and the University of Edinburgh. Upon coming to Texas in 1830, he took up land in Austin's Colony. Dr. Ewing was appointed chief surgeon of the Texas army and participated in the Battle of San Jacinto.

Death from starvation in Perote Prison, Mexico, was the lot of Irish-born Patrick Usher (1801-1843). As early as July 17, 1835, he had called a meeting of Lavaca-Navidad settlers at William Milligan's cotton gin for the adoption of a resolution calling for independence from Mexico. He fought at San Jacinto, served as chief justice of Jackson County, and represented that area in the 5th and 6th Congresses of the Texas Republic. A member of the Mier Expedition into Mexico, he was captured and imprisoned at Perote.

The commissary general of the Texas army was a County Cork man, John Forbes (1797-1880); he was serving as aide-de-camp to General Sam Houston when appointed to that office in April 1836. He had settled at Nacogdoches when he came to Texas in 1834 and was elected mayor of that town—an office he held for several years. Forbes was an attorney and surveyor and later served as lieutenant colonel on the staff of Governor Richard Coke.

Soldier in the revolution, architect for the national capitol at Houston when that city was the political center of the Republic of Texas, postmaster of the republic, chief clerk of the House of Representatives, three times mayor of Austin, commissioner of the General Land Office, United States consul at Panama, and collector of customs at the port of Corpus Christi—these were the activities and offices of Irish-born Thomas W. Ward (1807-1872). Educated as an architect, he left Ireland in 1828 and was practicing his profession in New Orleans when trouble erupted in Texas. He came here as a member of the New Orleans Greys and lost a leg at the Siege of Béxar. In 1841 he lost his right arm while firing a cannon to celebrate Texas independence. Ward was a Union supporter and a vehement opponent of secession. He died in Austin from typhoid fever.

Irishman James B. Shaw was a graduate of the University of Dublin and came to Texas in 1837, where he served a short term as a private in the army. He was made chief clerk of the Treasury Department in 1838 and, in 1839, was elected comptroller, serving in that office for 20 years. He became acting secretary of the treasury and, in 1850, was sent to Washington to collect the $5 million payment due Texas for relinquishing certain western land the republic had claimed. He again represented Texas in negotiations with the Federal government to settle the state's revenue debts.

Dublin-born William Kennedy served in 1842 as London consul of the Republic of Texas. He later served as British consul in Galveston. Kennedy had published a two-volume work on Texas. He obtained a contract to settle 600 families south of the Nueces River, but the colony was never established.

The Reverend John Anderson (1803-1884) was born at Dungannon, Ireland, and was educated at Belfast College. An educator and Presbyterian minister, he established Anderson Academy in Arkansas. In 1849 he moved to Clarksville, Texas, where he and his wife set up schools for boys and girls. His two sons served the Confederate cause.

Thomas Dwyer came to the United States at age 16. In 1849 he moved to Texas and opened stores at Quintana, Brazoria, Columbia, and Brenham. Active in Republican Party politics, he was, at one time, that party's nominee for governor. He died in 1876.

Orange, Texas, was the site of a shipyard established in the 1850's by an Irishman, Alexander Gilmer (1829-1906), who was born in County Armagh, Ireland. He had come to the United States in 1846. He owned and was operating several vessels on the Texas coast when the Civil War started. His ships successfully ran the Federal blockade several times. After the war he went into the sawmill business and owned a number of lumberyards in southeast Texas.

One of Texas's pioneer horticulturists was Irish-born William Watson (1835-1897). His work in that field, dealing particularly with peach and grape cultivation, won him the vice-presidency of the Texas Horticulturist Society and a place as a trustee of the Pomological Association in 1875. His publications

Dr. Alexander W. Ewing

Harry A. McArdle

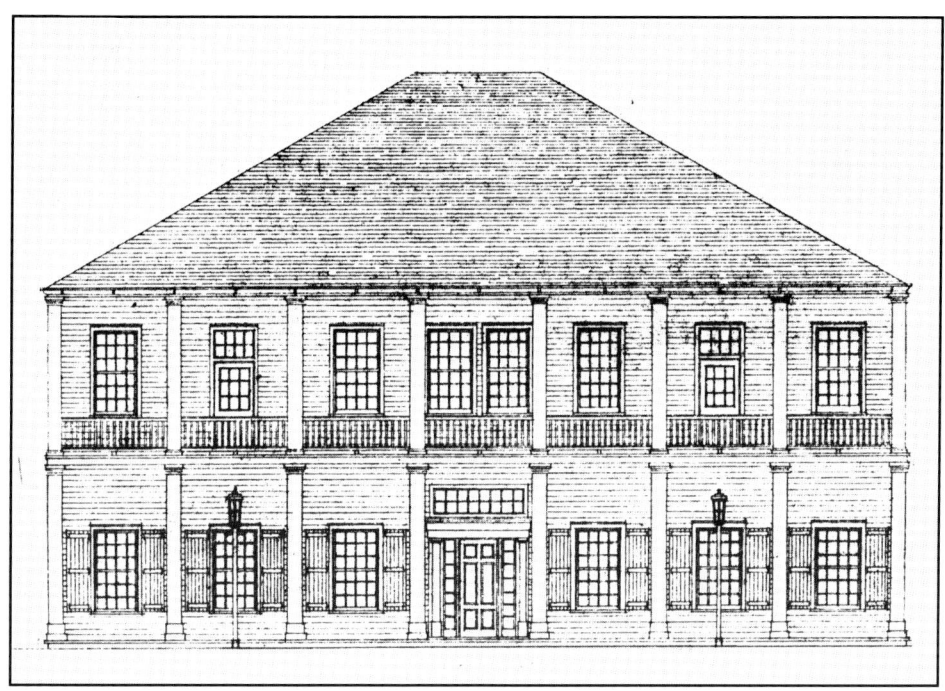
The Texas capitol at Houston, designed by Thomas W. Ward

included an early article on grape culture published in the 1869 *Texas Almanac*. He had come to Texas in 1859 and served in the Confederate army. Watson died at Brenham.

In the Senate chamber in Austin hang the paintings *Dawn at the Alamo* and *The Battle of San Jacinto* (see pages 10 and 74). These and other highly acclaimed works were painted by Irish-born Harry A. McArdle (1836-1908). In 1850 he came to the United States, where he continued the art studies begun in Ireland. In 1860 he won the Peabody Prize at the Maryland Academy of Design. During the Civil War, he served on the engineering staff of General Robert E. Lee. McArdle came to Texas in 1868 and, in 1870, was professor of art at Baylor Female College. He was employed by the state to paint various historical scenes and personages, and his paintings are known for their authenticity and attention to detail. McArdle spent his later years in San Antonio and died there.

Bishop Edward Joseph Dunne (1848-1910) was born in County Tipperary and came to Chicago with his family in 1849. He was ordained a Roman Catholic priest at Baltimore in 1871 and, in November of 1893, was consecrated Bishop of Dallas.

Rt. Rev. Alexander Charles Garrett, bishop of the Protestant Episcopal Diocese of Dallas (1874-1917), was born in County Sligo and educated at Trinity College in Dublin. Bishop Garrett typified the pioneering clergy in Texas. When he arrived in Dallas in 1874, he and five other clergymen ministered to a diocese that covered about 100,000 square miles in North and West Texas. Well known for his eloquence in the pulpit, his contemporaries called him the Chrysostom of the American Church.

Not All Wore White Hats

The Irish, as is true of all people, were to be found on both sides of the law. Some served as local lawmen; some rode with outlaw bands, and some with the Texas Rangers.

Whether a man was considered "on the side of the law" or an outlaw often depended on local circumstances or "how he played his hand." There was a thin line between the actions of the rancher and property owner who, for self-protection, had to take the law into his own hands and the violence of men like Sam Bass and John Wesley Hardin. King Fisher started out as a lawman chasing rustlers, became leader himself of a notorious band of rustlers, and later was sheriff of Uvalde County. Gambler Ben Thompson was elected city marshal of Austin, "gunned down" a gambler in another city, and, after trial for murder and acquittal, was given a hero's welcome back in Austin. The very ruthlessness of such men often made them effective lawmen.

Whether previously an outlaw or not, the lawman of a frontier society had to be ruthless in order to survive. There was little of the chivalric "code of the West" so emphasized by pulp magazines. The man foolish enough to walk out for the "street showdown" was apt to be shot from ambush.

The Texas Rangers, originally organized to curb Indian depredations, gained a reputation as an effective peacekeeping force. That reputation was based on ruthlessness and the fact that, unlike local lawmen, their authority was not limited by county or town limits. For many years theirs was the only state-level police body feared by outlaws. They attracted many recruits. Not all possessed the qualities of a Jack Hays, "Rip" Ford, or Leander McNelly. To the many good men on the force were added some who appear to have used the mask of Ranger authority for violence which, otherwise, would place them outside the law. A few of the commanders were probably of the same mold or simply inept as leaders. To one such, James Hughes Callahan, belongs the dubious honor of leading a band of Rangers who plundered and burned a Mexican town and almost precipitated an international incident.

Callahan had, as a member of the Georgia Battalion, fought under James Fannin at Coleto. He was spared at the Goliad Massacre and, after his release by the Mexicans, joined a Ranger unit. He saw action when, in 1842, Mexican General Woll invaded Texas. In 1855 he led three Ranger companies into Mexico in pursuit of Indians. He and his men crossed the border at Eagle Pass in October. He was met by a Mexican army unit some distance from the border, and, in his retreat, he and his men plundered and burned the town of Piedras Negras before recrossing the Rio Grande. He led a second raid into Mexico to recover some slaves and was then dismissed from the service.[1]

During the Cortina War in 1859, Captain W.C. Tobin led a band of Rangers from San Antonio to Brownsville to aid in the campaign against "The Red Robber of the Rio Grande." They distinguished themselves by storming the jail at Brownsville, taking from it a 65-year-old follower of Cortina and lynching him. Tobin's command, augmented to 250 men, then launched an attack on Cortina's ranch. They were ignominiously driven back to Brownsville by Cortina. While stationed at Ringgold Barracks on the Rio Grande, Tobin's men were accused of plundering the citizens in that area.[2]

The notorious Sam Bass seemingly started his career of crime under the tutelage of Joel Collins in 1877.

Bass had drifted to San Antonio, where many cattlemen were gathered to organize the spring cattle drive to the north. Collins, on behalf of the ranchers, was driving a herd to Deadwood, South Dakota, and hired Bass on as a cowboy. After the sale of the cattle, Collins gambled away the proceeds, so he and his cowboys held up stagecoaches in the Black Hills. Thus was Bass initiated to outlawry. However, stagecoach robbery was not very lucrative—and Collins still owed his friends back in Texas. The gang held up and robbed a Union Pacific train near a small town west of Ogallala, Nebraska. They were identified and were hunted from then on. Collins was killed, and Bass returned to Texas. Here he formed a gang that included Bill Collins, cousin of Joel, Jim Murphy, and a man with the Irish name of Herndon.

A series of train robberies by the gang put lawmen throughout the state on their trail. Murphy and Herndon were soon taken prisoner. Murphy, in return for special consideration for himself, agreed with authorities to betray Bass. He rejoined the gang, but Bass, alerted by friends suspicious of Murphy, intended to kill him. Another member of the gang, Frank Jackson—cousin to Murphy—vouched for him. When the opportunity presented itself, Murphy relayed word to the Rangers of a plan to rob the bank at Round Rock, 15 miles north of Austin.

In July 1878 Bass rode into Round Rock with Murphy, Jackson, and a fourth gang member named Barnes. On the pretext of getting feed for the horses, Murphy dropped off at a feed store, while the others rode on to the bank. They hitched their horses and walked into a store to buy some tobacco. There they were recognized by local deputies Moore and Grimes, who attempted to disarm them. Both lawmen were shot dead. The Rangers who had converged on the town, and who included Henry McGee and Chris Conner, joined in the gunfight. Barnes was killed. Bass and Jackson made a running fight of it. Bass was mortally wounded, but Jackson, holding off the lawmen with his pistol, helped his chief to his horse, and they shot their way out of town. As they galloped away, Jackson, who was holding the swaying Bass in the saddle, saw Murphy in the door of the feed store and swore he would kill him. The dying Bass was found the next day not far from the town. Jackson escaped.

When Murphy returned to his hometown of Denton, he learned that Jackson had been there looking for him. Now in fear for his life, he spent his time hanging around the sheriff's office for protection. Finally, the betrayer ended his life by drinking poison.[3]

During the 1870's the country between Castroville and Eagle Pass was reportedly ruled by King Fisher and his gang. They carried off cattle in broad daylight and, along the Nueces, maintained enclosed pastures where the stolen stock was kept until it could be marketed. Local authorities were helpless as the citizens were terrorized and would not inform.[4] The situation was much the same farther north and west.

The Rangers stepped into this maelstrom of lawlessness to bring order. Among those rounding up outlaws at this time were men like Ranger Lieutenant Pat Dolan and Sergeant O'Reilly. They "cleaned up" Kimble County with the arrest of 41 wanted men.[5] No doubt some of those apprehended also bore Irish names. Dolan was later given command of Company F of the Texas Rangers along the Nueces River.

One of the bloodiest gun battles involving Texas Rangers and outlaws occurred in East Texas in 1887. The outlaws, identified only as a family named Conner, were a gang composed of the father and "several stalwart sons." They lived in the "piney woods" of Sabine County.

The piney woods was an extensive area of thick timber, dense undergrowth, crisscrossing streams, and treacherous swamps. Close to the Texas-Louisiana border, it was an excellent hiding place for those fleeing the law and was a safe haven for the criminals who had decided to live there. From this impenetrable fortress, they sallied forth to prey on the law-abiding citizens of the surrounding territory. Anyone so foolhardy as to pursue the woodswise outlaws was liable to end up in a swamp or be blasted by a specially prepared load of buckshot. The shotgun, primed with a special handloaded charge, was a favored weapon in these deep woods, where any encounter was within a short range—usually only a few yards.

The Conners had for years terrorized the citizens of that part of Sabine County. Local law officers were ineffective against them, and the Rangers were called in.

A band of six Rangers, guided by an experienced woodsman, stalked the gang for a number of days. The gang changed their campsite daily, and it was evident that they were drawing the lawmen farther into the woods.

When the outlaws felt they had lured their pursuers far enough into

Pat Dolan

the woods, they prepared an ambush for them. The Rangers moved cautiously for-ward toward what appeared to be the Conners' campsite. Texas outlaws some-times used attack dogs, and, when the lawmen were within a few yards of the camp, the Conners loosed four vicious dogs on them. At the same time, they opened fire with rifles and shotguns. The latter were particularly devastating, since the pellets of the handloaded charges were held together by cooled wax. Ranger Jim Moore fell dead at the first volley, another Ranger was shot through the lungs, the Ranger sergeant was shot in both hands, and a fourth Ranger received a disabling wound in the side. In the exchange of gunfire, one of the Conners was killed, and another wounded and captured. The rest escaped as the Rangers, concerned with getting medical aid for their wounded, retired from the piney woods.[6]

In Conclusion

The Irish are still coming to Texas. According to the 1990 Federal census, there were then 2,630 Irish-born Texans residing in the state. The exact number of Texans with Irish antecedents is probably incalculable, but in the 1990 census, 2,368,958 Texans claimed Irish ancestry. They are scattered throughout the state, and Irish surnames are prominent in Texas's business, industrial, political, educational, religious, and civic life.

Where they are relatively numerous, they have formed Irish fraternal, social, and educational groups. Although differing in their programs and emphasis, a common thread runs through each group—a pride in Irish identity and culture and the adaptation of such to the benefit of their adopted state and community. San Antonio has three such organizations: The Irish Cultural Society of San Antonio, Inc.; The Harp and Shamrock Society of Texas; and a division of the Ancient Order of Hibernians and its Ladies' Auxiliary. There are three A.O.H. divisions in Houston and one in Abilene. In Corpus Christi and San Patricio, the Ladies' Auxiliary officially carries the A.O.H. standard. Dallas has a chapter of the Friendly Sons and Daughters of St. Patrick.

Small fraternal, social, or religious groups may have been organized among the early Irish Texans, but there was no nationally affiliated group until about 1874 when the first A.O.H. division was organized in Galveston. The city's populace included Hibernians who had moved from the Boston and Philadelphia areas, and most of the dockworkers were of Irish birth. By 1897 there were reported some 18 divisions in the state. By 1920 divisions were established across the state from Galveston and Houston to Dallas, Fort Worth, and Waco, and from there to Edinburg and El Paso in the west.

The principal reason for the A.O.H.'s existence in Texas appears to have been to provide aid, and sometimes housing, to the Irish immigrants who had continued to come here through the port of New Orleans and from the northern states. However, the organization's function as a link with the ancient history and culture was not overlooked. Minutes of now-defunct divisions list speakers on such topics as Irish history, ancient and modern, and Irish customs, traditions, and language.

In the 1920's restrictions were placed on immigration to America, and the decline began for the Ancient Order of Hibernians in Texas. World War II sounded the death knell for almost all the still-surviving divisions. The present resurgence of interest in Irish organizations, gathering momentum since the 1960's, is probably engendered by the realization of the possible loss of a unique identity. Why did the Irish Texans, most of whom had been here since the early 1800's, wait so long before organizing formal groups? Their countrymen in the north were organized almost from the time they set foot in the New World. The Friendly Sons of St. Patrick were well recognized in George Washington's time. He, during the Revolutionary War, had issued special St. Patrick's Day orders for the Irish contingents of the army.

The Irish who came to Texas came to a different world than did those who landed on the northeastern seaboard. On the American frontier, a man's religion and place of origin was of far less importance than his ability to handle a rifle and his willingness to give support to a neighbor. The Texas frontier did not yet have the established social, political, religious, and commercial institutions that feel themselves threatened by newcomers of a different national origin, religion, or economic status. In contrast to the settled and established societies of the North, the newcomers to Texas were welcomed and accepted for what they could contribute to a new order. The social and economic bars by which an established order strives to protect its status and privileges were not raised against them because there was no established order.

That "acceptance" did not cause the Irish immigrants to forget the country of their origin or lessen their pride in their "Irishness." This is evident in an examination of any of the old cemeteries where their tombstones can still be read. Occasionally the notations "Born in Ireland" or "Native of Ireland" will appear, but most often the Irish county of birth is noted. Frequently the parish or townland is also given. There are subtle differences between the Irish Texans and their countrymen of the North and Midwest. In the North the reaction to discrimination was the development of a "ghetto complex"—a hostile awareness of being set apart—and a defensive aggressiveness that made itself felt in political and commercial life and defied the establishment with organizations, parades, and demonstrations. There was no need of this in a Texas that accepted its immigrants at face value. In fact, acceptance and amalgamation as "Texans" was so complete that the descendants of those same immigrants ran the risk of a total loss of any ancient cultural identity. Perhaps a realization of this helped contribute to the proliferation of Irish societies in the late 1800's and their resurgence in the 1960's.

The River-Dyeing Festival, part of the St. Patrick's Day Celebration, San Antonio, 1978. A brilliant green dye is released from the barges into the San Antonio River, renamed River Shannon during the celebration. Members of the Harp and Shamrock Society of Texas and the Paseo del Rio Association, sponsors, ride on the barges while bagpipers play Irish tunes.

About the Author

John Brendan Flannery, who died in 1989, was a native of Ireland. He came to the United States at age 15, and Texas was his home from 1966 until the end of his life. He was an instructor in economics and international relations at St. Mary's University in San Antonio, Texas, at the time he wrote this book, and his other fields of interest included law, history, and socio-economic problems.

His writings include "Economics for the Layman," a presentation in simplified form of basic economic concepts; "El Tejano," an account of the contribution to Texas of the Spanish and Mexican Texan; *Reflections*, an examination of the philosophy of the credit cooperative movement; and "The Irish-World Citizens," a short account of Irish accomplishments in various countries.

Flannery served as president of the Irish Cultural Society of San Antonio, Inc., and *The Irish Texans* was as natural a consequence of his involvement with that organization as its publication in 1980 by the Institute of Texan Cultures was, and is in 1995, appropriate.

Acknowledgments

The pride of a Texan in Texas is no less well known than the pride of an Irishman in the Irish. Put the two together—an Irish Texan writing on the Texas Irish—and the work is anything but drudgery. However, many descendants of the Texas Irish have had a hand in developing *The Irish Texans*.

The necessary understanding of the pioneer Irish and their times evolved from the many hours of discussion with Mrs. Rachel Bluntzer Hébert and Hubert McGloin of Corpus Christi and San Patricio; Mrs. Irene Gallagher Peters, Mrs. Marguerite Mew Lowman and J. Patrick Dunne of Corpus Christi; Mrs. Hallie Fagan Snider of Tivoli and Refugio; Pat McGuill, Buck Emmert, and Mrs. Grace Fox Malone of Refugio; Maude and Mary Fox of San Antonio and Refugio; Grace Ryals of San Antonio; Miss Anne McKeown and Mrs. McWhorter of Beeville; Thomas Shelton of Refugio and San Antonio; John W. Meaney of Austin; and Mrs. Gilbert Vetters of Corpus Christi.

The correspondence, family records, business papers, and other reference materials so graciously provided were invaluable in depicting the lives and times of the colonists. For these I am indebted to Mrs. Hébert, Mrs. Snider, Mrs. Lowman, and Thomas Shelton. Finally, for some necessary corrections to parts of the manuscript, credit is due Mrs. Hébert and Pat McGuill. A sincere "thank you" to all.

John Brendan Flannery, 1979

1995 Addendum

The recent availability of a large number of historical photographs prompted the redesign and revision of the first edition of *The Irish Texans*. Photographic researcher and archivist Thomas Shelton located many of these images and obtained the accompanying caption material. He also made textual changes using research that has come to light since John Flannery first wrote the book. We thank him very much for his efforts.

We also thank the Institute's Mary Grace Ketner for her revision of the San Jacinto chapter and her research and rewriting of the Liberty-Beaumont chapter, again using newly available resources. Three other staff members went far above and beyond the call of duty to help us meet our deadlines: Lynn Catalina (and husband Ben), David Garrison, and Grace White. We are very grateful.

Several of our invaluable Institute volunteers updated the index for this edition, and we are immensely thankful for them! Darlene Murnin, in particular, contributed a great amount of time and effort, and Mary Burrow, June Deckard, and Anna Egger were also very helpful. We certainly appreciate their work.

And we are glad to have updated information on the Ancient Order of Hibernians in Texas compiled by Gerard P. Moran, A.O.H. state historian.

Sandra Hodsdon Carr, editor, 1995

Sources

Ashford, Gerald. *Spanish Texas.*
Baker, J.W. *A History of Robertson County, Texas.*
Bancroft, Hubert H. *History of Texas and the North Mexican States.*
Bauer, Grace. *Bee County Centennial 1858-1958.*
Binkley, William C. *The Texas Revolution.*
Bolton, Herbert E. *Texas in the Middle 18th Century.*
Brown, Dee. *Hear That Lonesome Whistle Blow.*
Brown, John Henry. *History of Texas.*
Bryant, Keith L., Jr. *History of the Atchison, Topeka and Santo Fe Railway.*
Caballero, Romeo Flores. *Counter-Revolution.* Trans. Jaime E. Rodriguez O.
Canales, José Thomas, ed. *Bits of Texas History.*
Castañeda, Carlos. *Our Catholic Heritage in Texas.*
Chabot, Frederick C. *With the Makers of San Antonio.*
Clarke, Thomas B., et al. *The American Railway.*
Connor, Seymour V. *Peters Colony of Texas.*
_____. *Texas in 1776.*
Cox, Mamie W. *The Romantic Flags of Texas.*
DAR, Alamo Chapter. *The Alamo Heroes and Their Revolutionary Ancestors.*
Davenport, Harbert. *The Angel of Goliad.*
Davis, Reverend Nicholas A. *The Campaign from Texas to Maryland.*
Ezell, Camp. *Historical Story of Bee County, Texas.*
Fehrenbach, T.R. *Lone Star: A History of Texas and the Texans.*
Gillett, James B. *Six Years with the Texas Rangers: 1875-1881.*
Grimes, Roy. *Goliad 130 Years After.*
_____, ed. *300 Years in Victoria County.*
Hatcher, M.A. *The Opening of Texas to Foreign Settlement 1801-1831.*
Hayes, Charles W. *History of the Island and the City of Galveston.*
Hollon, Eugene W., and Ruth Lapham Butler, eds. *William Bollaert's Texas.*
Huson, Hobart H. *El Copano—Ancient Port of Bexar and La Bahia.*
_____. *Refugio: A Comprehensive History of Refugio from Aboriginal Times to 1955.*
_____. *The Refugio Colony and Texas Independence.*
Kee, Robert. *The Green Flag.*
Kenney, M.M. *Recollections of Early Schools.*
Lamego, General M.A. Sanchez. *The Second Mexican-Texas War: 1841-1843.*
_____. *The Siege and Taking of the Alamo.*
Lawrence, Varuna Hartmann. *Texas Coastal Pioneers of Chambers County.*
Leybury, James G. *The Scotch-Irish.*
Linn, John J. *Reminiscences of Fifty Years in Texas.*
McComb, David G. *Houston: The Bayou City.*
McLain, Malcolm D., ed. *Papers Concerning Robertson's Colony in Texas.*

Mitchell, Mary Agnes. *The First Flag of Texas Independence*.
Molyneaux, Peter. *Romantic Story of Texas*.
Moody, T.W., and F.X. Martin, eds. *The Course of Irish History*.
Nacogdoches—Gateway to Texas.
Nance, Joseph M. *After San Jacinto*.
Nueces County Historical Society. *The History of Nueces County*.
Oberste, William H. *Texas Irish Empresarios and Their Colonies*.
———. *Our Lady Comes to Refugio*.
O'Connor, Kathryn Stoner. *Presidio La Bahia*.
Overton, Richard C. *Gulf to Rockies*.
Parker, Richard D. *Historical Recollections of Robertson County, Texas*.
Partlow, Miriam. *Liberty, Liberty County and the Atascosito District*.
Peña, José Enrique de la. *With Santa Anna in Texas*. Trans. Carmen Perry.
Pickett, T. Arlene. *Historic Liberty County*.
Red, William Stuart. *The Texas Colonists and Religion 1821-1863*.
Rives, George L. *The United States and Mexico*.
Rose, Victor M. *History of Victoria County*.
Scott, Florence J. *Historical Heritage of the Lower Rio Grande*.
Shannon, William V. *The American Irish*.
Sibley, Marilyn McAdams. *The Port of Houston, A History*.
Smith, W. Broadus. *Pioneers of Brazos County, Texas*.
Smylie, Vernon. *Taming of the Texas Coast*.
Sonnichsen, C.L. *Pass of the North: Four Centuries on the Rio Grande*.
Stambaugh, J. Lee, and Lillian Stambaugh. *The Lower Rio Grande Valley of Texas*.
Sterling, William Warren. *Trails and Trials of a Texas Ranger*.
Stratton, Florence. *The Story of Beaumont*.
Strobel, Abner J. *The Old Plantations and Their Owners of Brazoria County, Texas*.
Taylor, Paul Schuster. *An American-Mexican Frontier: Nueces County, Texas*.
Terrell, John Upton. *Apache Chronicle*.
Tolbert, Frank X. *The Day of San Jacinto*.
Turley, Sister Mary Immaculate, S.H.G. *Mother Margaret Mary Healy-Murphy*.
Webb, Walter Prescott. *The Texas Rangers: A Century of Frontier Defense*.
———, and H. Bailey Carroll, eds. *The Handbook of Texas*.
Weddle, Robert S., and Robert H. Thonhoff. *Drama and Conflict: The Texas Saga of 1776*.
Wharton Clarence. *Remember Goliad*.
Whipple, Judith. *Journal Letters and History of George W.K. Mew*.
Wittke, Carl. *The Irish in America*.
Wood, Alpha Kennedy. *Texas Coastal Bend: People and Places*.
Wooten, D.C. *A Comprehensive History of Texas*.
Xavier, Sister M., I.W.B.S. *A Century of Sacrifice*.
Yoakum, H. *History of Texas*.

Unpublished Manuscripts

"The Irish Empresarios of Texas," Sister James Joseph McBeath, C.C.V.I. Catholic University, 1953.
"Fr. Miguel Muldoon: The Story of an Early Pioneer Priest," Lina Trigg, St. Mary's University, 1940.
"Four Decades of Catholicism in Texas, 1820-1860," Sister Mary Angela Fitzmorris, A.M. Catholic University, 1926.
"A History of the O'Connor Ranch: 1834-1939," Sister Margaret Rose Warburton, C.D.P. Catholic University, 1939.

On file in the Library of the Institute of Texan Cultures:

"The Irish of Staggers Point," Mary Katherine Thompson Galloway.
"A Short History of the Byrne Family," James Byrne.
"My Family as I Remember Them," John H. Dunn, Corpus Christi, 1952.
"Young John," John W. Meaney, Austin.

Family Records

Correspondence, notes, family Bible entries, business records of pioneer members of the Fagan, Dougherty, and McGuill families in the possession, respectively, of Mrs. H.M. Fagan Snider of Tivoli, Texas; Mrs. Rachel Hébert of Corpus Christi, Texas; and Pat McGuill of Refugio, Texas.

Notes

San Jacinto

[1] John J. Linn, *Reminiscences of Fifty Years in Texas*, p. 264.
[2] Frank X. Tolbert, *The Day of San Jacinto*, p. 71, notes that the music that piped the Texans to battle was Thomas Moore's "Will You Come to the Bower"—an Irish air.
[3] William H. Oberste, *Texas Irish Empresarios and Their Colonies*, p. 217.

Why Were They Here?

[1] Robert Kee, *The Green Flag*, p. 19.
[2] Ibid., p. 43.
[3] Mercantilism, as practiced by leading European states, involved an economic practice implemented by political policy in colonial and conquered lands of repressing any development that would threaten home, industry, or markets. The English Corn Laws, part of this policy, discriminated against foreign-produced grains.
[4] James G. Leybury, *The Scotch-Irish*, pp. 158, 164.
[5] Ibid., p. 158.
[6] Kee, *Green Flag*, p. 123.
[7] Ibid., p. 247.

An Irish Conquistador and Others

[1] Robert S. Weddle and Robert H. Thonhoff, *Drama and Conflict: The Texas Saga of 1776*, p. 7.
[2] Seymour V. Connor, *Texas in 1776*, p. 7. Also see *The San José Papers: The Primary Sources for the History of Mission San José y San Miguel de Aguayo from Its Founding in 1720 to the Present, Part I: 1719-1791*. Trans. Fr. Benedict Leutnegger et al.
[3] John Upton Terrell, *Apache Chronicle*, p. 135.
[4] For an account of the weaknesses of New Spain's northern frontier and the prodigious remedial efforts of Oconór, see *Drama and Conflict* and *Texas in 1776* cited above.
[5] Weddle and Thonhoff, *Drama and Conflict*, p. 130.
[6] *Nacogdoches—Gateway to Texas*; see Bernadine Rice, "The Irish in Texas," in *Journal of the American Irish Historical Society*, vol. XXX, which notes a James Conilt in Texas in 1786.

[7]M.A. Hatcher, *The Opening of Texas to Foreign Settlement 1801-1831*, pp. 14, 16.
[8]Carlos Castañeda, *Our Catholic Heritage in Texas*, vol. V, p. 315.
[9]Hatcher, *Opening of Texas*, p. 102.
[10]Castañeda, *Our Catholic Heritage*, vol. V, p. 316.
[11]Hatcher, *Opening of Texas*, p. 178.

Irish Mexicans

[1]Romeo Flores Caballero, *Counter-Revolution*, p. 24.
[2]José Enrique de la Peña, *With Santa Anna in Texas*, p. 148.
[3]The ability to extemporaneously compose poetry to suit the occasion was required of the ancient Irish *filidh* and was thus much admired in Ireland. Father Muldoon apparently cultivated this talent. See Lena Trigg, "Fr. Miguel Muldoon: The Story of an Early Pioneer Priest," master's thesis, St. Mary's University, 1940.

The Father Muldoon toast was found among the papers of Colonel Guy M. Bryan, according to "Notes and Fragments," *Quarterly of the Texas State Historical Association*, vol. II, p. 243.
[4]Edna Rowe, "The Disturbances at Anahuac, 1832," *Quarterly of the Texas State Historical Association*, vol. VI, p. 266.
[5]See "The Prison Journal of Stephen F. Austin," *Quarterly of the Texas State Historical Association*, vol. II, p. 198, and Abner J. Strobel, *The Old Plantations and Their Owners of Brazoria County, Texas*, p. 23.
[6]D.G. Wooten, *A Comprehensive History of Texas*, p. 130, describes Father Muldoon as a man of warm heart and a social and generous spirit who will be long held in grateful remembrance by the old settlers of Texas.

Although Father Muldoon is associated with the Austin colonies, William Stuart Red in *The Texas Colonists and Religion, 1821-1863*, p. 51, notes that this priest had, in 1829, "commenced to officiate in the colony of San Patricio but withdrew because the colony did not grow." He may also have "withdrawn" because the San Patricio colony already had its own priest—Father Henry Doyle.

The "Non-Irish" Colonies

[1]See Lester G. Bugbee, "Old Three Hundred," *Quarterly of the Texas State Historical Association*, vol. I, p. 108.
[2]Wooten, *Comprehensive History*, p. 103.
[3]M.M. Kenney, "Recollections of Early Schools," *Quarterly of the Texas State Historical Association*, vol. I, p. 285.

[4] Richard D. Parker, *Historical Recollections of Robertson County, Texas*, p. 12, and J.W. Baker, *A History of Robertson County, Texas*, p. 29. See also pp. 31, 59, 97, and 103 for other references to the Staggers Point Irish.

[5] "The Irish of Staggers Point," an unpublished account by Katherine Thompson Galloway and others, contains a listing of the original settlers and the account of Bryant's defeat.

[6] Seymour V. Connor, *The Peters Colony of Texas*, p. 107.

[7] Walter Prescott Webb and H. Bailey Carroll, eds., *The Handbook of Texas*, vol. I, p. 456.

[8] Connor, *Peters Colony*, pp. 169-440.

The Irish Empresarios

[1] Oberste, *Texas Irish Empresarios*, p. 91, and Alpha Kennedy Wood, *Texas Coastal Bend: People and Places*, p. 26.

[2] Oberste, *Texas Irish Empresarios*, p. 94.

[3] Testimony of Mrs. Rosalie B. (Hart) Priour, Welder vs. Lambert in Refugio County District Court, 1896, as reprinted in the *Bicentennial Edition, Refugio County Press*, August 4, 1976.

[4] Wood, *Texas Coastal Bend*, p. 29; Oberste, *Texas Irish Empresarios*, p. 24.

[5] Kathryn Stoner O'Connor, *Presidio La Bahia*, p. 225.

[6] Wood, *Texas Coastal Bend*. Contradictory accounts are given of McGloin's birthplace in Ireland as being County Sligo and County Leitrim. Hubert McGloin of Corpus Christi identifies the birthplace as being near Castlegal. This village is almost on the county line separating the two counties. On a visit in 1978, the author went to the area. There are McGloins on both sides of the line, but the building identified as the farmhouse birthplace of James McGloin, now renovated and modernized, is in County Sligo.

The San Patricio Colony

[1] William H. Oberste, *Our Lady Comes to Refugio*, p. 51.

[2] Bauer, *Bee County*, p. 96.

[3] Camp Ezell, *Historical Story of Bee County, Texas*, p. 17. The name "Poesta," according to Mrs. Rachel Hebert of Corpus Christi, was originally "Paiste," presumably an Indian word and used by old-time Mexicans to mean "moss." Change of place-names over time is not unusual. That part of Texas known now as the Melon Ranch was originally the Malone or Melone Ranch.

[4] Oberste, *Texas Irish Empresarios*, p. 116.

[5] Sister James Joseph McBeath, C.C.V.I., "The Irish Empresarios of Texas," dissertation, Catholic University, 1953.

⁶Ibid.
⁷Ezell, *Historical Story of Bee County, Texas*, p. 6.
⁸Ibid., p. 9. See also reminiscences of Patrick Burke as published in the *Beeville Bee*, January 12, 1912.
⁹Ibid., p. 16.
¹⁰McBeath, "Irish Empresarios of Texas."

The Refugio Colony

¹In a letter dated September 7, 1837, to his son, Martin Power of Refugio, Daniel Power in Ireland mentions the burden of the "tythes" still being paid. (This was eight years after passage of the Catholic Emancipation Act.) Letters and copies in the possession of Thomas Shelton of Refugio and San Antonio.
²Hobart H. Huson, *The Refugio Colony and Texas Independence*, p. 4. Page 14 of Wood's *Texas Coastal Bend* states Power "gained about 350 recruits."
³"A History of the O'Connor Ranch: 1834-1939," Sister Margaret Rose Warburton, C.D.P., dissertation. Catholic University, 1939. A Power colonist, William St. John, cited by Oberste in *Texas Irish Empresarios*, p. 109, stated that "probably one-third of the people who started with me from Ireland . . . died of cholera. . . ." Mrs. Rosalie (Hart) Priour, testifying in a District Court case in Refugio County, stated that "about 250 colonists died and were buried at sea. . . ."
⁴McBeath, "Irish Empresarios of Texas."
⁵Oberste, *Texas Irish Empresarios*, p. 110.
⁶Huson, *Refugio Colony*, p. 94.
⁷McBeath, "Irish Empresarios of Texas."
⁸Ibid.
⁹Ibid.

Everyday Life in the Colonies

¹Mrs. T.C. Allen, "Reminiscences of Mrs. Annie Fagan Teal," *Southwestern Historical Quarterly*, vol. XXXIV, p. 317.
²"Progenitors," a reprint of a 1934 account by J.C. Heard in the *Bicentennial Edition, Refugio County Press*, August 4, 1976.
³Allen, "Reminiscences of Mrs. Teal," p. 319.
⁴For description of water sources and house construction and materials, see Oberste, *Texas Irish Empresarios*, p. 142.
⁵See the reminiscences of Patrick Burke, *Beeville Bee*, January 12, 1912.
⁶Allen, "Reminiscences of Mrs. Teal."
⁷Reminiscences of Patrick Burke, *Beeville Bee*, January 12, 1912.
⁸Ibid.

[9] "Progenitors," a reprint of a 1934 account by J.C. Heard.
[10] Warburton, "O'Connor Ranch."
[11] Mary Agnes Mitchell, *The First Flag of Texas Independence*.
[12] Oberste, *Texas Irish Empresarios*, p. 234.
[13] Ibid., p. 144.
[14] Reminiscences of Patrick Burke, *Beeville Bee*, January 12, 1912.
[15] See account by Merle Kelly as told to Judge T.W. McGuill and printed in the *Bicentennial Edition, Refugio County Press*, August 4, 1976.
[16] Warburton, "O'Connor Ranch."
[17] See account by E.R. "Scrub" Kelley, *Bicentennial Edition, Refugio County Press*, August 4, 1976.
[18] Interview with Mrs. D. McWhorter, Beeville. See also John Dunn, "My Family as I Remember Them," for the country in 1851 being "open country, mostly prairie," and John W. Meaney, "Young John," where it is noted: "By this time (1877) the grassy prairie was being damaged by inroads of mesquite."
[19] Allen, "Reminiscences of Mrs. Teal."
[20] Information on family religious observances from interviews with Mrs. Hallie M. Fagan Snider, Tivoli; Pat McGuill, Refugio; Mrs. Rachel Bluntzer Hébert, Mrs. Irene Gallagher Peters, and Patrick J. Dunne of Corpus Christi.
[21] On February 17, 1838, one James C. Allen wrote an order to James Power to pay the bearer $60 worth of goods for 20 head of cattle.

In 1841 Patrick Fitzsimmons at Liberty, Texas, in a letter to Martin Power at Live Oak, notes "no money in this place" and tells of working for a blacksmith in return for shirts and clothing. He also wrote of trading "corn, potatoes and fodder" for two horses, and that the blacksmith let him have a cow and a calf which, with some hogs, he wanted to trade for a horse. From Power's documents, in copies and originals, in possession of Thomas Shelton of San Antonio and Refugio.

Barter was a common practice until well into the 1870's as indicated by other family records of Nueces area settlers.

Two Would-Be Texas Towns and a Texas Frontier Storekeeper

[1] Many settlements that had played important roles in 19th century Texas have declined or disappeared. To Blanconia and Gussettville might be added Staggers Point, St. Marys, San Patricio, Indianola, and others.
[2] See Clara V. O'Brien, "Old-Time Storekeeper—Civilization's Advance Scout," *Frontier Times*, September 1970.
[3] In *Taming of the Texas Coast*, Vernon Smylie gives this remarkable woman's real name as Sarah Jane Newman.

[4]Most of the Blanconia data was obtained through Pat McGuill of Refugio from family records and data in his possession.

Pro-Mexican Irish?

[1]As noted by T.R. Fehrenbach in *Lone Star: A History of Texas and the Texans*, "Planters and men of property did not want war. Few of the Old Three Hundred desired independence." See pp. 174-89 for development of the independence movement. A short-sighted Mexican Centralist policy drove the Peace Party to join the War Party.

T. Arlene Pickett in *Historic Liberty County*, p. 25, notes that there were a number of people who lived in Texas who "desired to live a peaceful life" and "did not consider war a means to an end."

[2]Peter Molyneaux, *Romantic Story of Texas*, p. 225, and Frederick C. Chabot, *With the Makers of San Antonio*, with reference to Seguin.

[3]The pertinent points of the San Felipe Declaration are noted by Molyneaux in *Romantic Story of Texas*; it was a firm insistence on certain rights but not an action of revolt. The other extremes were represented by the conciliatory Columbia and Gonzales Resolutions and Travis's attack on Anahuac.

[4]See James McGloin, "Fighting in the Irish Colonies," and William G. Cooke, "The Matamoros Expedition," pp. 35 and 42 respectively, in José Thomas Canales, ed., *Bits of Texas History*.

[5]Allen, "Reminiscences of Mrs. Teal," p. 327.

[6]Oberste, *Texas Irish Empresarios*, p. 274.

[7]Florence J. Scott, *Historical Heritage of the Lower Rio Grande*, p. 130.

[8]Hobart H. Huson, *Refugio: A Comprehensive History of Refugio County from Aboriginal Times to 1955*, vol. I, p. 229, and Nueces County Historical Society, *The History of Nueces County*, p. 35.

[9]Huson, *Refugio County from Aboriginal Times*, vol. I, p. 229.

[10]Oberste, *Texas Irish Empresarios*, p. 162.

[11]Ibid., p. 179.

[12]Camp Ezell, in *Historical Story of Bee County, Texas*, p. 22, notes a few of the San Patricio colonists who died in the Goliad Massacre. A memorial column in the Old San Patricio Cemetery lists seven San Patricians who died in the Goliad Massacre.

[13]Huson, *Refugio Colony*, p. 2, lists seven San Patricians in the Goliad Massacre.

[14]Ibid., p. 4.

[15]Oberste, *Texas Irish Empresarios*, p. 186.

The First Skirmishes

[1] Huson, *Refugio County from Aboriginal Times*, vol. I, p. 212, and Hubert H. Bancroft, *History of Texas and the North Mexican States*, vol. II, p. 222.
[2] Huson, Refugio County from Aboriginal Times, vol. I, p. 216.
[3] Nueces County Historical Society, *History of Nueces County*, p. 35, notes that Refugio responded with 24-25 men under Power. See also Huson, *Refugio County from Aboriginal Times*, vol. I, p. 218.
[4] Bancroft, *History of Texas*, vol. II, pp. 221-22, and Nueces County Historical Society, *History of Nueces County*, p. 35.
[5] Ibid., p. 36.
[6] Huson, *Refugio County from Aboriginal Times*, vol. I, p. 229.
[7] Ibid., p. 226, and Bancroft, *History of Texas*, vol. II, p. 224.
[8] Webb and Carroll, *Handbook of Texas*, vol. 1, p. 700.
[9] These local men are listed by Roy Grimes in *300 Years in Victoria County*, p. 118; Ezell in *Story of Bee County*, p. 22, lists the Irish noted; Oberste, *Our Lady*, lists additional names, p. 65.
[10] Mitchell, *First Flag*, pp. 7 and 10. This publication carries an appendix of copies of the "Morning Reports" of the Goliad troops under Captain Dimmitt. For accounts of other flags, see Mamie W. Cox, *The Romantic Flags of Texas*.

The Santa Anna Campaign

[1] Wooten, *Comprehensive History*, p. 222.
[2] Huson, *Refugio County from Aboriginal Times*, vol. II, p. 287.
[3] Bancroft, *History of Texas*, vol. II, p. 22.
[4] "The Story of the Alamo," a pamphlet published by the Daughters of the Republic of Texas, contains the names and origins of the Alamo heroes. To the list of Irish-born has been added the name of Edward McCafferty, who, although given no place of origin in the pamphlet, was an Irish colonist from San Patricio. See also *The Alamo Heroes and Their Revolutionary Ancestors*, a Bicentennial Project of the Alamo Chapter, DAR.
[5] Huson, *Refugio County from Aboriginal Times*, vol. 1, p. 287.
[6] Oberste, *Texas Irish Empresarios*, p. 199.
[7] Bancroft, *History of Texas*, vol. II, p. 22.
[8] Clarence Wharton in *Remember Goliad*, p. 40, notes King and his men were captured March 14. See Roy Grimes, *Goliad 130 Years After*, p. 65.
   According to Harbert Davenport in *The Angel of Goliad*, they were killed March 16.
[9] Hobart H. Huson, *El Copano: Ancient Port of Bexar and La Bahia*, p. 31.

[10]Grimes, *Goliad*, p. 94.
[11]Wharton, *Remember Goliad*, p. 48.
[12]Oberste, *Texas Irish Empresarios*, footnote p. 216, lists all of those noted except Matthew Byrne, John Fadden, Edward Ryan, and Edward Garner—names listed on a San Patricio Cemetery memorial to the San Patricio dead at Goliad.

None Paid a Greater Price

[1]Huson, *Refugio County from Aboriginal Times*, vol. II, p. 281.
[2]Allen, "Reminiscences of Mrs. Teal," p. 325.
[3]William C. Binkley, *The Texas Revolution*.
[4]Fehrenbach, *Lone Star*, p. 245, and Molyneaux, *Romantic Story*, p. 356.
[5]*Telegraph and Texas Register*, August 23, 1836.
[6]*Telegraph and Texas Register*, October 26 and November 30, 1836.
[7]John M. Nance, *After San Jacinto*.
[8]H. Yoakum, *History of Texas*.
[9]Nueces County Historical Society, *History of Nueces County*, p. 48.
[10]*Telegraph and Texas Register*, June 1, 1842.
[11]See "Friction on the Frontier" in Paul S. Taylor, *An American-Mexican Frontier, Nueces County, Texas*.
[12]Oberste, *Texas Irish Empresarios*, p. 52.
[13]Ezell, *Story of Bee County*, p. 19.
[14]Ibid., p. 7, and Oberste, *Texas Irish Empresarios*, p. 145.
[15]Letter of James McGloin to J.W. Bowers quoted by Oberste, *Texas Irish Empresarios*, p. 179.
[16]Ibid., p. 234.
[17]O'Connor, *Presidio La Bahia*, pp. 260-64.
[18]Oberste, *Texas Irish Empresarios*, p. 234.
[19]Warburton, "O'Connor Ranch."
[20]*Victoria Advocate, Historical Edition*, 1968, sec. 11, p. 19.
[21]Bauer, *Bee County*, p. 5.
[22]Warburton, "O'Connor Ranch." During the years 1836-1850, Indians raided westward from the Colorado River. Webb, in *Texas Rangers*, writes of a Ranger unit clashing with Comanches in 1837 near present-day Austin and, in 1839, of three Ranger companies being organized under Colonel John Moore on the Colorado to meet the Comanche threat.
[23]Oberste, *Texas Irish Empresarios*, p. 227.
[24]Ibid., p. 235.
[25]Ibid., pp. 241-42.
[26]General M.A. Sanchez Lamego, in *The Second Mexican-Texas War: 1841-1843*, notes that 2,150 were designated, at the end of 1841, for a thrust into Texas.

[27] Ibid., p. 19.
[28] Wooten, *Comprehensive History*, p. 387.
[29] Oberste, *Texas Irish Empresarios*, p. 251.
[30] Ibid., pp. 242-43. For general accounts of the chaotic conditions on the Texas frontier, see Nance, *After San Jacinto*; Taylor, *American-Mexican Frontier*; and Nueces County Historical Society, *History of Nueces County*.

The Irish of Victoria

[1] Grimes, *300 Years in Victoria*, p. 115.
[2] Taylor, *American-Mexican Frontier*, p. 14.
[3] *Victoria Advocate, Historical Edition*, 1968, sec. II, p. 7.
[4] Ibid. See also Grimes, *Goliad*, p. 108, which gives Mexican General Urrea's account of seizing flour, sugar, rice, and potatoes at Linnville for distribution to his men. Linn's warehouse there was probably the source of most of the seized goods.
[5] *Victoria Advocate, Historical Edition*, 1968, sec. IV, p. 2.
[6] "Reminiscences of Mrs. Elizabeth McAnulty Owens," originally written by Mrs. James F. Welder and reprinted in the *Victoria Advocate, Historical Edition*, sec. II.
[7] James Byrne, "Short History of the Byrne Family," unpublished account.
[8] Victor M. Rose in his *History of Victoria County* gives biographical sketches of the early settlers of that area.
[9] Grimes, *300 Years in Victoria County*.

Disturbances in the Irish Colonies, 1835-1852

Most of the dates given for the incidents are agreed upon by Texas historians. However, where no date has been specified or where contradictory ones are noted, that date or time is given which is most plausible and in accord with other related and recorded circumstances.

Texas Irish and the Civil War

[1] See Nicholas A. Davis, *The Campaign from Texas to Maryland*, for listings of personnel of Texas regiments in various Civil War engagements.
[2] Charles W. Hayes, *History of the Island and City of Galveston*, vol. II, pp. 556-57; note McCormick's account of the Battle of Galveston Bay.
[3] Interview with Mrs. Hallie M. Fagan Snider of Tivoli, Texas.
[4] Webb and Carroll, *Handbook of Texas*, vol. I, p. 517; vol. II, p. 525.

The Irish of San Antonio

[1] Chabot, *Makers of San Antonio*, p. 348, and Webb and Carroll, *Handbook of Texas*, vol. II, p. 813.
[2] Ibid., vol. I, p. 661.
[3] Chabot, *Makers of San Antonio*, p. 50. See *San Antonio Light*, July 8, 1912, concerning Bryan Callaghan's son.
[4] Chabot, *Makers of San Antonio*, p. 322, and Webb and Carroll, *Handbook of Texas*, vol. I, p. 530.
[5] Chabot, *Makers of San Antonio*, p. 292, and Webb and Carroll, *Handbook of Texas*, vol. I, p. 557.
[6] Chabot, *Makers of San Antonio*, p. 322, and Webb and Carroll, *Handbook of Texas*, vol. I, p. 495.
[7] For a description of the Irish Flats, some surnames of Irish settlers, and their way of life, see the *San Antonio Express*, February 23, 1908; *San Antonio Express Magazine,* September 11, 1949; *San Antonio News*, October 15, 1965; and *San Antonio Light*, September 6, 1969.

The Irish of the Corpus Christi Area

[1] Interview with Patrick J. Dunne of Corpus Christi.
[2] Nueces County Historical Society, *History of Nueces County*, p. 56.
[3] Sister Mary Xavier, I.W.B.S., *A Century of Sacrifice*, p. 5.
[4] Ibid., p. 10.
[5] Ibid., p. 13.
[6] From lists of elected city and county officials provided by Corpus Christi City Secretary Bill Read and Judge Robert Barnes.
[7] Interview with Mrs. Marguerite Mew Lowman of Corpus Christi.
[8] Interview with Mrs. Irene Gallagher Peters of Corpus Christi.
[9] Judith Whipple, *Journal Letters and History of George W.K. Mew*.
[10] Interview with Mrs. Irene Gallagher Peters of Corpus Christi.
[11] Interview with Mr. John W. Meaney, Austin.
[12] Documents in possession of Mrs. Rachel Bluntzer Hébert, Corpus Christi.
[13] Dunn, "My Family as I Remember Them," and Meaney, "Young John." Copies of these unpublished accounts in the possession of John W. Meaney of Austin, Texas.
[14] Meaney, "Young John," p. 22. For political and commercial activities of some Irish-surnamed people in the Brownsville and Rio Grande area, see J. Lee Stambaugh and Lillian Stambaugh, *The Lower Rio Grande Valley of Texas*.

The Liberty-Beaumont Areas

[1] Marian Partlow, *Liberty, Liberty County and the Atascosito District*, pp. 65-126.
[2] Christine Moor Sanders, *Captain George Washington O'Brien and the History of the Gladys City Company at Spindletop.*
[3] Partlow, *Liberty*, p. 126.

Irish Railroaders and Houston-Galveston

[1] Richard C. Overton, *Gulf to Rockies*, p. 27.
[2] Thomas B. Clarke et al, *The American Railway*, p. 431.
[3] Dee Brown, *Hear That Lonesome Whistle Blow*, p. 65.
[4] Webb and Carroll, *Handbook of Texas*, 2 vols.
[5] Marilyn McAdams Sibley, *The Port of Houston: A History*, pp. 89-100, and David G. McComb, *Houston: The Bayou City*, p. 78.
[6] Keith L. Bryant Jr., *History of the Atchison, Topeka and Santa Fe Railway*, p. 127.
[7] Ibid., p. 129.
[8] Charles W. Hayes, *History of the Island and City of Galveston*, vol. II, p. 902.
[9] Ibid., p. 914.
[10] Dubose Murphy, "Early Days of the Protestant-Episcopal Church in Texas," *Southwestern Historical Quarterly*, vol. XXXIV, p. 300. See also Hayes, *History of the Island*, vol. II, p. 869.
[11] Ibid., vol. II, p. 966.
[12] Ibid., p. 978.
[13] Ibid., p. 979.

All of God's Children

[1] There were orders of nuns in Texas prior to 1892; however, all were long-established and of non-Texan origin.
[2] The author has relied heavily on the biography of Mother Margaret Mary Healy Murphy by Sister Mary Immaculata Turley, S.H.G., for this account.

Honorable Mention

The examples given of contributions of Irish to the independence, politics, public administration, and other aspects of Texas life are taken from Webb and Carroll, *Handbook of Texas*.

Not All Wore White Hats

[1] Webb, *Texas Rangers*, p. 146.
[2] Ibid., pp. 182, 187. See also Fehrenbach, *Lone Star*, p. 514.
[3] See James B. Gillett, *Six Years with the Texas Rangers: 1875-1881*, p. 108, for the account of the Bass gang.
[4] Webb, *Texas Rangers*, p. 286.
[5] Ibid., pp. 328, 332, and Gillett, *Six Years*, p. 132.
[6] William Warren Sterling, *Trails and Trials of a Texas Ranger*, p. 309.

Photographic Credits

All prints are from the collections of The University of Texas Institute of Texan Cultures, courtesy of the following lenders. Credits of photographs positioned left to right are separated by semicolons, from top to bottom by dashes.

Page 2	Joseph Perkins, *A New General Atlas*, 1824.
Page 4	The Institute of Texan Cultures.
Page 5	The Institute of Texan Cultures.
Page 8	Sue Flanagan Collection, First Presbyterian Church, San Angelo.
Page 10	Texas State Capitol, Austin. Copy courtesy State Preservation Board, Austin.
Page 11	Andrew Jackson Houston, *Texas Independence* (Houston: Anson Jones Press, 1938). Copy courtesy Library of the Daughters of the Republic of Texas at the Alamo.
Page 16	The *San Antonio Light* Collection, The Institute of Texan Cultures.
Page 17	James H. Sutton Jr., San Antonio.
Page 18	The Center for American History, The University of Texas at Austin.
Page 22	D. Vicente Riva-Palacio, *Mexico, a Través de los Siglos* (Mexico City: Ballasca y Comp., 1887-1888).
Page 23	The Institute of Texan Cultures.
Page 27	Mrs. Sam Rice, Bryan.
Page 31	Hobart Huson, *Refugio*, (Woodsboro: Rooke Foundation, 1953-1955). Courtesy Kathleen Huson Maxwell–Estate of Jamie Lambert Hynes, Refugio.
Page 33	Both from Thomas F. Shelton, San Antonio.
Page 38	Celeste Hopkins Brown, Victoria.
Page 39	Catholic Archives, Corpus Christi–Thomas F. Shelton, San Antonio.
Page 42	Thomas F. Shelton, San Antonio.
Page 44	Estate of Jamie Lambert Hynes, Refugio.
Page 45	Janie O'Brien Harkins, Refugio–Our Lady of Refugio Church, Refugio. Courtesy Maxine Reilly.

Page 46	Estate of Madie Mitchell Simmons, Refugio.
Page 50	Estate of Roger Fleming, Woodsboro—Allie Burke Young, Refugio.
Page 52	Celeste Hopkins Brown, Victoria—Estate of Isabella Mitchell Shelton, Refugio.
Page 54	Louise O'Connor, Victoria.
Page 55	Hallie Fagan Snider, Tivoli—Refugio County Courthouse, Refugio. Courtesy Stephen E. Scanio.
Page 56	Estate of Jamie Lambert Hynes, Refugio.
Page 58	Allie Burke Young, Refugio.
Page 59	Ann McGuill Hawkins, Temple.
Page 61	Both from Ann McGuill Hawkins, Temple.
Page 65	Alexander Dienst Collection, The Center for American History, The University of Texas at Austin.
Page 71	Estate of Jamie Lambert Hynes, Refugio.
Page 72	Mary Agnes Mitchell, *The First Flag of Texas Independence*, (Refugio, 1937).
Page 74	Texas State Capitol, Austin. Copy from The Institute of Texan Cultures.
Page 80	Mrs. C.B. McWhorter, Beeville.
Page 81	Mary Corrigan Walker, San Antonio; Thomas F. Shelton, San Antonio.
Page 82	Estate of Roger Fleming, Woodsboro.
Page 85	The Center for American History, The University of Texas at Austin.
Page 86	Estate of Jamie Lambert Hynes, Refugio.
Page 90	Cecile Morris Price, Victoria—Henry Hauschild Jr., Victoria.
Page 92	Martha Elizabeth Owens Staley Martin, San Antonio; Estate of Jamie Lambert Hynes, Refugio.
Page 93	Julia Keefe Gillean, Victoria.
Page 94	Julia Keefe Gillean, Victoria.
Page 98	*Frank Leslie's Illustrated Newspaper*, January 24, 1863.
Page 99	Lawrence T. Jones, Confederate Calender Works, Austin.
Page 100	*Harper's Weekly*, September 1863.
Page 102	Both from the Witte Museum, San Antonio.
Page 103	Elizabeth Conroy Gibson, San Antonio;Archives Division, Texas State Library, Austin.
Page 104	The *San Antonio Light* Collection, The Institute of Texan Cultures.
Page 105	Mary Ann Noonan Guerra, San Antonio.
Page 108	Marion Uehlinger, Corpus Christi
Page 109	The Library of the Daughters of the Republic of Texas at the Alamo, San Antonio.
Page 110	Catholic Archives, Corpus Christi; Marguerite Mew Lowman, Corpus Christi—Irene Gallagher Peters, Corpus Christi.
Page 113	Rachel Bluntzer Hébert, *The Forgotten Colony: San Patricio de Hibernia* (Burnet: Eakin Press, 1981).
Page 115	Thomas F. Shelton, San Antonio.
Page 116	John W. Meaney, Austin.
Page 118	Thomas F. Shelton, San Antonio.
Page 119	Chilton O'Brien, Beaumont.
Page 123	Houston Metropolitan Research Center, Houston Public Library, Houston.
Page 124	Mrs. Nicholas J. Clayton Jr., La Marque—Rosenberg Library, Galveston.
Page 129	Both from the Sisters of the Holy Spirit, San Antonio.

Page 130   The Sisters of the Holy Spirit, San Antonio.
Page 131   The Sisters of the Holy Spirit, San Antonio.
Page 135   Both at top from Archives Division, Texas State Library, Austin—
           Harris County Heritage Society, Houston.
Page 136   The Center for American History, The University of Texas at Austin.
Page 140   Western History Collections, University of Oklahoma, Norman.
Page 143   The *San Antonio Light* Collection, The Institute of Texan Cultures

Index

Italic numerals indicate photographs.

Agua Dulce Creek, Battle of 11, 73, 95
Alabama 26
Alamo, Battle of 11, 66, *074*
Albion (ship) 36
Aldrete, José 36
Allen, Martin 25
Almonte, Juan N. 9
Anahuac 23, 117
Ancient Order of Hibernians 141, 142
Anderson Academy 134
Anderson, Rev. John 134
Annexation Convention 30
Apache Indians 15, 16, 17, 51, 79, 83, 96
Aragon, Volunteer Regiment of 15
Aransas City 84, *85*, 96
Aransas Creek 37, 79, 81, 114
Aransas National Wildlife Refuge 95
Aransas Pass 30, 37, 43
Argyle Hotel *104*, 104
Arizona (ship) 100
Arkansas 134
Asquith, Lord 3
Atascosito 117
Atchison, Topeka, and Santa Fe Railroad 123
Austin 83, 87, 112, 134, 136, 137, 139, 145
Austin, Stephen F. 22, 23, 26, 32, 66
Austin, Stephen F. Colony 21, 25, 26, 63, 64, 71, 133
Australia 34
Austria 13
Ballygarrett, County Wexford, Ireland 29, 41
Baltimore, Maryland 32, 136
Banquete 66
Barnard, Joseph Henry 67
Barnes (surname) 139
Barr, William 18
Barragan (surname) 21
Barragan, Marcos 21
Barragan, Miguel 21
Barrett, Timoteo 19
Barry, H.N. 107
Bass, Sam 137, 138, 139
Battle of San Jacinto, The 10, 136
Baylor Female College 136
Bayou City (ship) 97, 98, 100
Beaumont 99, 117-20
Beaumont *Journal* 120
Bee County 37
Beeville 60, 62, 80, 145
Belfast, Ireland 18
Belfast College 134
Bell County 122
Benavides, Placido 91
Benchley 27
Benchley, Henry W. 27
Berrigan (surname) 21
Béxar 19, 63
Béxar, Siege of 70, 71, 101, 118, 134
Bexar County 101, 103
Béxar Presidio: see San Antonio
Black Hills, South Dakota 138
Blain, Thomas 18

Blair, Samuel 43
Blair's Landing, Battle of 99
Blanc, Bishop 32
Blanco Creek 58, 59, 60
Blanconia 57, 58, 60, *61*, 62
Book of Brands 55
Borland, Margaret Heffernan *38*, 38
Boston, Massachusetts 141
Boyd, William 125
Boyle, Andrew 76
Boyle, Joseph 28
Boyne River, Battle of the 13
Bracken, William 70
Brady, John Thomas 122
Bray, James 43
Bray, Patrick 87
Brazoria 121, 134
Brazos 63
Brazos County 121
Brazos River 12, 27
Brenan family 121
Brenham 134, 136
Brien, Catherine 28
"Brinon on the Moor" (song) 121
Brittany 1
Browin, Bryan 19
Brown, James 37, 43
Brownsville 131, 138
Bryan 121
Bryan, Christopher 118-20
Bryan, John N. 28
Bryan family 121
Bryant, Benjamin 12, 27
Bryant's Defeat (battle) 27
Buckley family 104
Buffalo Bayou 7, 84
Buffalo Bayou Ship Channel Company 122, *123*
Burke (de Burgo) (surname) 3, 120
Burke, Mrs. Ann 37
Burke, James *65*, 87
Burke, Patrick 37, 51
Burke, William 43
Burke's Hollow 86
Burnet, David G. 9, 78
Burnet, Mrs. David G. 9
Burns, Samuel E. 74
Byrne, James W. 76, 93
Byrne, Matthew 76
Byrne, Peter 92
Byrnes, James 78
Cahill, Cornelius *110*
Cahill, Cornelius, family 109, 111
Cahill, Johanna 111
Cahill, Michael 87
Caldwell County 121
California 17, 129
Callaghan (surname) 25
Callaghan, Alfred 102
Callaghan, Bryan V., Jr. 102
Callaghan, Bryan V., Sr. 102
Callaghan, S.D. 37
Callaghan, Stephen W. 28
Callahan 121
Callahan, James Hughes 138
Callihan, Charles 107

Campo Santo de la Parroquia de Santiago del Saltillo 32
Canales, Antonio 85, 87, 96
"Capitan Colorado:" see Hugo Oconor
Carey 122
Carlisle, James 38
Carlisle, L. 37
Carlisle, Robert 38
Carolinas 13
Carroll, George W. 120
Carroll, Mrs. Mary 37
Carroll, Pat 37
Carter, Charles 37
Casey, Harvey 28
Casey, John, 28
Casey, John, Jr. 28
Casey, John, Sr. 28
Casey, Thomas 28, 79
Casey, Timothy 28
Cash, George W. 76
Cassidy, Thomas 28
Cassidy, Thomas, Sr. 28
Cassidy, William 12
Castañeda, Francisco 69
Castroville 105, 139
Catholic Emancipation Act 41
Cattle brands 55
Chambers, Thomas Jefferson 23
Childress County 122
Civil War 60, 93, 94, 97-100, 102, 103, 111, 113, 115, 119, 121, 122, 123, 125, 128, 134, 136
Clare, Eliza 37
Clare, H.T. 37
Clareville 37
Clark (surname) 25
Clarksville 134
Clary, Elisha C. 28
Clary, Elisha T. 28
Clay, Clement 103
Clayton, Nicholas J. *124*
Cleary, Dr. John, family 109
Clifton (ship) 102
Coahuila y Texas, Province of 63
Coke, Richard 133
Coleto Creek, Battle of 11, 75, 76, 81, 91, 95, 138,
Collin County 27
Collins, Albert G. 28
Collins, Bill 138
Collins, Joel 138
Collins, John H. 28
Collins, Thomas 28
Collins family 104
Columbia, Texas 134
Comanche Indians 15, 53, 81, 83, 84, 96
Conely, Cornelius 28
Conilt, James 18
Connaught, Ireland 18
Connecticut 103
Conner, Chris 139
Conner family 139, 140
Connor, Joseph W. 28
Connor, William D. 28
Constitution of 1824 63, 64, 71

163

Constitution of 1845 30
Constitution of 1876 109
Consultation of 1835 30, 71, 89
Convention of 1836 30, 32, 67
Convention of 1845 30
Convention of 1875 129
Conway, John 28
Cooke County 27
Copano 31, 36, 37, 42, 43, 58, 69, 70, 75, 95
Copano Bay 30, 35, 36, 37, 41
Cork, Ireland 101
Corn Laws 14
Cornegay, Francisco 18
Corpus Christi 1, 51, 57, 79, 89, 107-16, 128, 129, 134, 141
Corpus Christi *Star* 107
Corrigan, John 37, 79
Corrigan, Ellen O'Toole 79, 80, *81*, 114
Corrigan ranch 95
Cortina, Juan M. 138
Cortina War 138
Cos, General Martin Perfecto de 64, 67, 69, 70, 71, 95
Cosgrove family 104
Council House Fight 83
County Antrim, Ireland 89
County Armagh, Ireland 134
County Cork, Ireland 124, 128, 133
County Derry, Ireland 133
County Donegal, Ireland 113
County Down, Ireland 124
County Dublin, Ireland 124
County Fermanagh, Ireland 58
County Galway, Ireland 99, 124
County Kerry, Ireland 34, 111, 124, 129
County Kilkenny, Ireland 32
County Leitrim, Ireland 58, 124
County Limerick, Ireland 128
County Mayo, Ireland 37, 118, 124
County Queens, Ireland 124
County Roscommon, Ireland 58
County Sligo, Ireland 34, 38, 114, 124
County Tipperary, Ireland 37, 124, 136
County Waterford, Ireland 103
County Westmeath, Ireland 101, 111, 124
County Wexford, Ireland 29, 41, 46
Cowen, Hugh 28
Coyle, Hugo 19
Craven, David 37
Croix, General Teodoro de 18
Cuba 15
Cuchullen 49
Cummings (surname) 25
Cummings, Elizabeth 34
Cummins (surname) 26
Dallas 27, 28, 109, 120, 123, 136, 141, 142
Dallas County 27
Davis (surname) 3
Davis, Jefferson 103
Davis, Joshua 43
Davis Guards 99, 100, 125
Dawn at the Alamo (painting) 74, 136
Deadwood, South Dakota 138
De Burgo (surname) 3
Declaration of Independence, Goliad 64, 71, 91

Declaration of Independence, Texas 30, 64
Delaney, Dan 28
De León, Martin 26, 89, 91
De León Colony 25, 26, 91
Denton 139
Denton County 27
De Solis, Fray Gaspar José 16
Devine, James M. 102-103
Devine, Thomas J. 102-103, *103*
Devine, William 102
DeWitt Colony 25, 63
Dillon (surname) 3
Dillon family 104
Dimmitt, Phillip 64, *65*, 70, 71, 72, 85, 96
Dixon, Mary Fullerton Henry 26
Dixon, James M. 26
Dog Branch Creek 59
Dolan, Pat 139, *140*
Dolan family 104
Dooley, George W. 28
Dooley, James 28
Dooley, William 28
Dorsey, Alfred 75, 76
Dougherty, James 113
Dougherty, Rachel 114
Dougherty, Robert Francis *113*, 113, 114, 115
Dougherty family 113
Dougherty residence *115*
Dowling, Richard W. (Dick) *99*, 99, 100, 125
Downey family 104
Doyle, Father Henry 36, 37
"Drill, Ye Tarriers, Drill" (song) 121
Dublin, Ireland 3, 15, 102, 118, 125, 133
Dubuis, Bishop Claude-Marie 128
Duffy family 104
Dungannon, Ireland 134
Dunn, Anne 112
Dunn, Isabella 26
Dunn, James 26
Dunn, John (Refugio colonist) 43, 65, 70, 77
Dunn, John, Jr. 112, 116
Dunn, John, Sr. (of Corpus Christi) 107, 109, 116
Dunn, John (son of "Red John") *116*
Dunn, John, family 109, 115
Dunn, John B. "Red John" *116*
Dunn, Lawrence 115
Dunn, Mary 107
Dunn, Matt 115
Dunn, Matthew 12, 107, 109
Dunn, Mike 116
Dunn, Patrick 107
Dunn, Peter 107, 109, 114
Dunn, Peter, family 109
Dunn, Thomas 107, 109
Dunn family 115
Dunne, Bishop Edward Joseph 136
Dunne, J. Patrick 114
Dunne family 115
Dutchtown 108
Duval County 113
Duvalt, Andrew 74
Dwyer, Edward 102
Dwyer, Simon, family 37

Dynne (surname) 114-15
Eagen, Mrs. Brigid 93
Eagle Pass 138, 139
Eaton, Rev. Benjamin 125
Edinburg, Texas 142
El Paso 98, 141, 142
Elliott, William 102
Emmert, Buck 62
Emmet (surname) 3
"Emmet's Speech from the Dock" (oration) 105
England 1, 13, 14, 15
English Act of Union 1
Espada Mission 54
Episcopal Church 125
Evans, Robert 74
Evergreen Cemetery 92
Ewing, Alexander W. 133, *135*
Fadden, John 76
Fadden, Pat 37
Fagan, John 53, 70, 76, 77, 81
Fagan, Joseph 54
Fagan, Mary 51
Fagan, Nicholas 43, 53, 70, 71, 72, 76, 77, 81, 98
Fagan, Oscar G. 55
Fagan, Peter 53, 55, 98, 99
Fagan family 53
Fagan settlement 47, 50
Fannin, James W. 66, 73, 74, 75, 76, 77, 90, 91, 95, 138
Fayette County 24
Fear, James, family 19
Feely, James, family 109
Filisola, General Vicente 84
Findley, Jeremiah 87
Fisher (surname) 114
Fisher, King 137, 139
Fitzgerald (surname) 3, 25
Fitzgerald, Edward 87, 107
Fitzgerald, Father James 108
Fitzgerald, Martha 120
Fitzgerald, Patricio 19
Fitzgerald, William 19
FitzSimmons, John 87
FitzSimmons, Joseph 109
FitzSimmons, Joseph, family 109
Foley, Henry 77
Foley, Dr. Henry 120
Forbes, John 133
Ford, John Salmon (Rip) 138
Fort Lipantitlán 30, 66, 70, 71, 85, 95, 96
Fort Merrill 51
Fort Sabine 99, 100
Fort Sam Houston 106
Fort Stockton 101
Fort Worth 123, 142
Fort Worth and Denver Railroad 122
Fourth of July celebrations, Irish 51
Fox, Christopher 125
Fox, James 87
Fox, John 87
Fox, Michael 43, 87
Fox family 46, 52
France 13, 93, 128
Frazer, Hugh McDonald 75
Friendly Sons and Daughters of St. Patrick 141
Friendly Sons of St. Patrick 142

Fullerton, George H. 26
Fullerton, Henry 26
Fullerton, Sarah 26
Fullerton, William 26
Galán, Bonifacio 36
Gallagher, E.J. 130
Gallagher, John 111
Gallagher, Mrs. Richard 111
Gallagher, Richard, family 109, 111
Gallagher, Peter 101, *103*
Gallagher, William 28
Galveston 91, 97-99, 121-25, 134, 141, 142
Galveston, Battle of 97-99, *98*
Galveston Bay 97, 117
Galveston Bay and Texas Land Company 117
Galveston County 125
Garaghty, Patrick 39
Garner, Edward 76
Garrett, Rt. Rev. Alexander Charles *136*
Garrett family 26
Garza, Carlos de la 67, 69, 76
Gates, Lewis 76
General Consultation: see Consultation of 1835
General Council 30, 32
George West 59
Georgia Battalion 75, 138
Gilleland, Johnson [Johnstone], family 83
Gilmer, Alexander 134
Gladys City Oil, Gas and Manufacturing Company 120
Gleeson, John 76
Glorieta Pass, Battle of 98
Goliad *17*, 36, 64, 65, 66, 67, 69, 70, 71, 73, 74, 75, 76, 81, 84, 85, 86, 90, 95, 96
Goliad, Battle of 11, 66, 67, 71, 76, 90, 96, 138
Goliad Declaration of Independence: see Declaration of Independence, Goliad
Goliad Flag of Independence 64, 71
Gonzales 64, 69, 74, 77, 83
Gonzales, José Manuel 86, 87, 96
Gould, Jay 123
Grant, James 64, 73, 95
Grayson County 27
"Great Comanche Raid" 83
Greece 49
Griffith (surname) 3
Grimes (surname) 139
Guadalupe River 1, 11, 12, 64, 77, 78
Guajardo, Josefa: see Josefa Guajardo Hewetson
Gulf, Colorado and Santa Fe Railway 122, 123
Gulf of California 17
Gulf of Mexico 77, 94, 120
Gussett, Norwick 57
Gussettville *50*, 57, 58
Haley family 91
Hardin, John Wesley 137
Harp, Jack 138
Harp and Shamrock Society of Texas 141
Harriet Lane (ship) 97, *98*
Harrisburg, Texas 121

Harrisburg and San Antonio Railway 125
Hart, Abraham 28
Hart, Caleb 28
Hart, Felix 38
Hart, Jacob 28
Hart, James 51, 84, 96
Hart, Luke 37
Hart, Mary 37-38
Hart, Pat 38
Hart, Timothy 37-38, 43, 65, 84
Hart, William J. 28
Haskell County 122
Hawkins, Joseph M. 74
Hayes, Patrick 37
Hays, John 83
Hays, John Coffee (Jack) 101
Healy, Jane 128
Healy, Margaret Mary: see Margaret Mary Healy Murphy
Healy-Murphy Center 131
Hearn, Daniel B. 28
Hearn, Martin 28
Hearn, William A. 28
Hearne 121
Hearne, Robert Patrick 43
Hébert, Mrs. Rachel Bluntzer 111
Hefferman (surname): see Heffernan
Heffernan, James 37, 80
Heffernan, John 37, 38, 80
Heffernan, Margaret: see Margaret Heffernan Borland
Heffernan family 38, 80, 95
Hennessey, P.H. 125
Henry, Elizabeth (Mrs. Hugh) 26
Henry, Elizabeth (Mrs. Robert) 26
Henry, Hugh 26
Henry, James A. 26
Henry, Robert 12, 26
Henry, William 26
Herndon (surname) 138
Hertzberg Collection, San Antonio 34
Hessian mercenaries 14
Hewetson, James 29, 30, *31*, 32, 38, 44, 46, 86
Hewetson, Josefa Guajardo 32
Hidalgo County 121
Hidalgo Seminary 113
Higgins 122
Higgins, G.H. 122
Higgins, John 28
Higgins, Lewis T. 28
Higgins, Pattillo 120
Higgins, Philemon 28
Higgins, William 28
Higgins family 26
Hood's Texas Brigade, Co. F, Fifth Texas Infantry Reg. 119
Houston 1, 9, 23, 77, 98, 99, 100, 121-25, 134, 141, 142
Houston, Sam 7, 9, *10*, 12, 24, 30, 73, 74, 75, 91, 118, 133
Houston and Texas Central Railroad 123
Houston Belt and Magnolia Park Railway Company 122
Houston Direct Navigation Company 122
Howard, Joe 81, 82
Hughes (surname) 25
Hughes, Charles R. 125

Hughes, Patrick 93, *94*
Hunter, William L. 76
Hutchinson, Charlotte Gallagher, residence *110*
Hynes, John 84
Hynes, Peter 77
Hynes Spring 84
India 114
Indian Territory 123
Indianola 56, 57
Indians 15, 16, 17, 23, 26, 27, 37, 48, 51, 53, 78, 79, 80, 81, 82, 83, 84, 95, 106, 121, 138; see also tribes, Apache, Comanche, Karankawa
Ireland in 1824 *2*
Irish at the Battle of San Jacinto 12
Irish at the Battle of the Alamo 74
Irish at the Battle of the Nueces 87
Irish at Villa Santísima Trinidad de Salcedo 19
Irish colonies and other areas of Irish settlement 4-5
Irish colonists' marker *42*
Irish Cultural Society of San Antonio 141
Early Irish settlers in Bee County 37
Irish Flats 104-106
Irish founding families of Old St. Patrick's Church, Corpus Christi 109
Irish from San Patricio who died at Coleto Creek and Goliad 76
Irish in Lipantitlán Battle 70
Irish in Peters Colony 28
Irish Original Settlers of Staggers Point 26
Irish Potato Famine 34
Irishtown 108
Iturbide, Agustín de 21
Jackson, Alexander 25
Jackson, Frank 139
Jackson, Humphrey 25
Jackson, William D. 74
Jackson County 133
James, George 114
James, John 76, 114
Jefferson County 117
Jenkins Ferry, Battle of 99
John, Emma E. 120
Johnson, F.W. 73
Johnson County 27
Kansas City, Mexico and Orient Railroad 122
Karankawa Indians 80, 84, 96
Keenan, Thomas 28
Kelly (surname) 25
Kelly, E.R. "Scrub" 51
Kelly, John 43, 75, 76, 79
Kelly, Charlotte, "Auntie" 111-12
Kelly, Martin, family 109
Kelly, Merle 51
Kelly, R.E. 120
Kennedy (surname) 25
Kennedy, Calvin W. 28
Kennedy, James 28
Kennedy, John 28
Kennedy, Mary 28
Kennedy, Samuel 28
Kennedy, William 134
Kenney, M.M. 26
Kerr, David 37

Kerrigan, Arthur 28
Killeen 122
Killeen, Frank P. 122
Killely, Mark 37
Kimble County 139
King, Amon 75, 95
Kinney, Henry L. 108, 111
Kinsale, Battle of 13
La Bahía (presidio) 17, 36, 64, 70, 91
La Grange 24
Lamar Peninsula 92
Lambert, James 70
Lambert, John 70
Lambert, Walter 12, 44, 69, 70, 84, 87
Lambert family 46
Lampasas 123
Laredo 131
Laughlin, James P. 28
Laughlin, Newton C. 28
Laughlin, William B. 28
Lavaca Bay 91
Lawlor, Martin 70
Lee, Robert E. 136
Liberty 117-20
Liberty County 117-20
Liberty Volunteers 117
Linn, Edward 87
Linn, John J. 9, 26, 52, 66, 70, 77, 89-91, 90
Linn, John Jr. 91
Linn, Mrs. John J. 91
Linnville 83, 96
Lipan Indians: see Apache Indians
Lipantitlán: see Fort Lipantitlán
Lipantitlán, Battle of 30, 70, 90, 95, 96
Lipscomb County 122
Little Bird (Indian chief) 81
Little Brazos River 26
Live Oak Point 32, 69, 84, 85
Liverpool, England 34, 42, 115
Lockhart 83
Logan, W.H. 118
London, England 134
Louisiana 19, 41, 42, 56, 77, 117, 118, 131, 139
Lucas Gusher 120
Lunn, Juan, family 19
Lynch (surname) 25
McArdle, Henry A. 10, 74, 135, 136
MacArty, Augustine 19
McBride, James 28, 107, 108
McBride, James, family 108, 109
McBride, Mary Dunn: see Mary Dunn
McCafferty, Edward 74
McCarthy, Augustine: see Augustine MacArty
McCarty, Gerard 28
McCarty, Larkin 28
McCarty, William, Jr. 28
McCarty, William, Sr. 28
McClary, Patrick 28
McCormick (surname) 25
McCormick, A.J. 120
McCormick, Arthur 9, 25
McCormick, Michael 9, 98
McCormick, Peggy 9, 11, 25, 98
McCormick League 7, 11
McCormick marsh 8
McCowan (surname) 114
McDermott, Joseph B. 28

McDermott family 104
McDonough, Edward 43, 77, 78
McDonough, Michael 70
McElroy, John C. 28
McFaddin, James 117-18
McFaddin, James, family 117
McFaddin, William M. 118
McFaddin, W.P.H. "Perry" 118
McGee, Henry 139
McGee, James 74
McGloin, Edward 37
McGloin, Elizabeth Cummings: see Elizabeth Cummings
McGloin, James 29, 32, 33, 34, 36, 37, 44, 66, 67, 91, 129
McGloin, James residence 33
McGloin, John 37, 76
McGloin, Mary Murphy: see Mary Murphy
McGloin, Patrick 37
McGloin house 113
McGowan, Dennis 76
McGuill, Martin 60, 61, 62
McGuill, Mary O'Reilly 59
McGuill, Thomas 58, 59, 59, 60, 62
McGuill, William 12, 58
McGuill family 46, 60, 62
McGuill, Thomas and Mary, home, gathering at 61
McGuill settlement 62
McGuill store 61
McGuire, Captain 114
McKeown, James, residence 39
McKinney, Robert 74
McMahan 121
McMillan, Ann 26
McMillan, Edward 12
McMullen, Esther Cummings 32
McMullen, John 29, 32, 34, 36, 37, 46, 84, 91
McMullen-McGloin colonists 38
McNamara, J. 28
McNelly, Leander H. 138
McNulty, James 18
Maconilt, James 18
Macool, Finn 49
Macool, Ossian 49
McSheany, John 37
Maeve, Queen 49
Magee, Juan, family 19
Magruder, John 97, 99
Mahan, Patrick 26, 87, 92
Mahan, Thomas 92
Mahon, John 93, 93
Malone, Charles 12, 70
Malone, John 43
Malone, Perry 28
Maloney, John 28
Manehuila Creek 76
Manihan, Charles 28
Manning, Delilah C. 28
Manning, John 28
Mansfield, Battle of 99
Maryland Academy of Design 136
Matagorda 36
Matamoros, Mexico 23, 32, 34, 64, 66, 73, 84, 85, 102, 127, 128
Meaney, John W. 112
Messenger (ship) 37
Mexican War 128

Mexico 15, 17, 21, 32, 34, 60, 63, 64, 66, 67, 70, 73, 84, 85, 86, 87, 92, 95, 101, 102, 103, 115, 117, 131, 133, 138; see also New Spain
Mexico City 23
Mier Expedition 92, 133
Milam County 121
Milligan, William 133
Mississippi 131
Missouri, Kansas, and Texas Railroad 122
Molloy, Father John T. 37, 73
Monahans 121
Monclova, Mexico 32
Montague County 27
Moody, John E. 52
Moody, W.L. 123
Moore (surname) 25, 139
Moore, Jim 140
Moore, John H. 69
Moran 122
Moran, John J. 122
Moran family 104
Morfi (surname) 18
Morfi, Father Juan Agustín 18
Morgan, George, family 26-27
Morphy (surname) 18
Moses 41
Mount Calvary Cemetary, Refugio 32, 33
Muldoon 24
Muldoon, Father Miguel 21-22, 23, 24
Muldoon, Father Miguel, marker 23
Mulroney, John 19
Munster, Ireland 18
Muro, Father Miguel 36
Murphy, (surname) 18
Murphy, Eli 28
Murphy, Henderson 28
Murphy, James 75
Murphy, Jerome 79
Murphy, Jim 138-39
Murphy, Johanna 129
Murphy, John 128
Murphy, John B. 128, 129
Murphy, Margaret Mary Healy 127-31
Murphy, Mary 34
Murphy, Thomas G. 28
Murray, Ambrose R. 28
Murray, Daniel 28
Musquiz, Ramon 43
Mustang Island 42
Nacogdoches 18, 19, 63, 133
Navarro, José Antonio 102
Neptune (ship) 97
Neraz, Bishop John Claudius 130
Neven, Patrick 76
New Houston City Company 122
New Mexico 98
New Orleans, Louisiana 26, 30, 34, 35, 37, 42, 43, 56, 89, 93, 99, 100, 125, 127, 134, 142
New Orleans Greys 76, 134
New Packet (ship) 36
New Spain 13, 15, 17, 18
New Washington 9
New York, New York 19, 32, 35, 36, 111, 123
Nolan, Christopher 28
Nolan, Philip 18

Noonan, George Henry *105*
Normans 3
North Carolina 57
Northern Ireland 13-14
Nova Scotia 103
Nowlan, James 74
Nueces, Battle of the 86, 87
Nueces Bay 30
Nueces County 107, 129
Nueces River 30, 31, 37, 50, 57, 66, 70, 78, 79, 80, 95, 108, 128, 134, 139
Nuecestown 108
Nuestra Señora de Loreto: see La Bahia (presidio)
Nuestra Señora del Refugio Mission 36, 59, 75, 91, 95
O'Boyle, Daniel 38
O'Boyle, Patrick 37
Obregon (surname) 21
Obregon, Ignacio 21
Obregon, Joaquin 21
O'Brien 122
O'Brien (surname) 21
O'Brien, Elizabeth Power 41, 43
O'Brien, George W. 118-20, *119*
O'Brien, Isabella (Elizabeth) 43
O'Brien, Morgan 65, 70, 71, 87
O'Brien, Thomas 41
O'Brien, Thomas John 49, 70, *71*, 75
O'Brien family 46, 53
O'Brien homestead (Refugio County) *50*
O'Connor, Dennis 53
O'Connor, Hugh: see Hugo Oconór
O'Connor, James 12, 37, 70
O'Connor, Mary Fagan: see Mary Fagan
O'Connor, Thomas Marion 12, 51, 70, 87, *92*
O'Connor family 46, 53, 54
O'Connor Ranch 54
Oconór, Hugo 15-18
Oconór, John 18
O'Docharty, George, family 37
O'Docharty, Patrick, family 109
O'Docharty, William 36
O'Donnell, Michael 65
O'Donoghue (surname) 18
O'Donoghue, Juan: see Juan O'Donojú
O'Donojú (surname) 18
O'Donojú, General Juan 21, 22
O'Driscoll, Daniel 12, 70, 87
Ogallala, Nebraska 138
O'Grady, Alice 104
O'Grady, Robert Emmit 104
O'Hara, John 28
O'Keefe, Michael 55, 93
Oklahoma 27
Old Irish Church 26
Old St. Mary's 58
Old San Fernando Cemetery 101
Old Three Hundred 25
Oliver, Andrew 93
O'Loughlin family 114-15
O'Neal, William 28
O'Neil, Martin 28
O'Quinn, Leonida 28
O'Quinn, Stephen 28
O'Quinn, William 28
Orange 134
Ordinance of Secession, 1861 97

O'Reagan (surname) 93-94
O'Reilly (surname) 139
O'Reilly, Father Bernard 108, 109, *110*
O'Reilly, James 70
O'Reilly, Michael 70
O'Reilly, Patrick 70
Oso Creek 111
Oso Ranch 111
O'Toole, Jeremiah 37, 70
O'Toole, John 38, 70
O'Toole, Martin 12, 38, 114
O'Toole, Michael 38
O'Toole family 114
Our Lady of Refuge Church 45
Our Lady of the Rosary Church 59, 60
Owasco (ship) 97
Owens, Elizabeth McAnulty 91, *92*
Padre Island 85, 96
Pajarita de Sangre *81*, 81
Palo Alto, Battle of 98
Panama 134
Panhandle and Santa Fe Railroad 122
Papalote Creek 37
Papalote Creek Settlement 47
Parker County 27
Parnell (surname) 3
"Pat Malloy" (song) 121
Payton, John R. 26
Payton, Sarah 26
Pecos County 101
Penescal Ranch 116
Pennsylvania 119, 123
Perilous Trails of Texas, The 116
Perote Prison 101, 133
Perry, Edward 76
Peters, Mrs. Irene Gallagher 111
Peters Colony 25, 28
Philadelphia, Pennsylvania 30, 32, 46, 141
Piedras Negras, Mexico 138
Pike, Zebulon 19
Pleasant Hill, Battle of 99
Plum Creek, Battle of 83
Poesta Creek 37, 47, 80
Poesta Creek settlement 47
Pomological Association 134
"Poor Paddy He Works on the Railroad" (song) 121
Port Sullivan 121
Portilla, Don Felipe Roque de la 30
Portilla, Dolores de la 30
Powder Horn (Indianola) 56
Power (de Poer) (surname) 3
Power, Dolores de la Portilla: see Dolores de la Portilla
Power, James 29-32, 33, 41, 43, 44, 69, 70, 71, 81, 84, 86, 87, 96
Power, James, tombstone *33*
Power, John 43
Power, Martin 43, 77
Power, Tomasa de la Portilla 31, 32, 84, 85
Power-Hewetson Colony 38, 44, 46
Power residence, Copano *31*
Power residence, Live Oak Point 85
Powers, Richard 107
Powers, Richard, family 109
Priour, Rosalie Hart 30
Prudence (ship) 42

Pugh, Thomas 37
Quin, M. 125
Quinn (surname) 70
Quinn, James 26, 91
Quinn, John 70
Quinn, Michael 70
Quinn, Miguel 19
Quinn, Mrs. James 91, 92
Quinn, Patrick 37, 38, 70
Quinn, Thomas 76
Quinn, William 37-38, 75, 76, 91
Quinn family 91-92
Quintana 134
Quiñones, Agatón 85, 96
Quirk, Bridget 38
Quirk, Edmund 12, 77
Quirk, Thomas 76
Ragan, George W. 28
Ramón family 102
Ranahan, James, family 109
"Recollections of Early Schools" (article) 26
Red River 27
Redmond, William 12
Red Top Prairie 26
Refugio 1, 25, 32, *33*, 36, 43, *44*, *45*, 50, 51, *52*, 60, 62, 66, 74, 75, 77, 79, 82, 83, 85, 86, 93, 95, 96
Refugio, Battle of 11,
Refugio Colony 29, 30, 36, 41-46, *42*, 47, 67, 69, 70, 77, 79, 98
Refugio County 46, 54, 55, 56, 60, 84
Refugio Mission: see Nuestra Señora del Refugio Mission
"Reminiscences of Mrs. Anne Fagan Teal" (article) 78
Republic of Texas 46
Revolution, Texas 26, 30, 46, 63-87
Revolutionary War, American 14, 118, 142
Rice, Jimmie H. 26
Riggs, Mary Heffernan *80*, 107
Ringgold Barracks 138
Rio Grande 18, 71, 78, 83, 84, 89, 107, 138
Roark, William M. 28
Robertson Colony 25
Robertson County 26, 121
Rock Pass 86
Rodriguez, Nicholas 66, 67
Rome, Italy 49
Round Lake *33*, 113, *115*
Round Rock 139
Rusk, Jackson J. 74
Rusk, Thomas J. 91
Ryals, Henry 86, 96
Ryan (surname) 80
Ryan, Edward 76
Ryan, Henry 37
Ryan, John, family 37
Ryan, William 70
Rylie, James R. 28
Sabine County 139, 140
Sabine Pass 99, 100
Sabine Pass, Battle of 99-*100*
Sabine River 117
Sabriego, Manuel 67, 69
Sachem (ship) 99, 100
"Sacking of Refugio" 85
Sacred Heart Academy, Waco 130

Sacred Heart of Jesus, Consecration to 54
St. Anthony's Chapel 54
St. Catherine's Church 60, 62
St. Charles Bay 93
St. Dennis Chapel 54
St. Hyacinth, Plain of 7
St. Joseph Island 42, 43
St. Joseph's Catholic Church, Gussettville 57, *58*
St. Joseph's Catholic Church, San Antonio 129
St. Joseph's School and Convent, San Patricio 38-*39*
St. Louis, Missouri 109
St. Mary's Catholic Church, San Antonio 106
St. Patrick's Catholic Church, Corpus Christi 108, *109*
St. Patrick's Catholic Church, San Antonio 106
St. Patrick's Catholic Church, San Patricio 38
St. Patrick's Day 142, *143*
St. Vincent's Cemetery 100
St. Peter Claver Church, San Antonio *130*
Salado Creek, Battle of 26
Saltillo, Mexico 30, 32
San Antonio 1, 15, 16, 18, 19, 26, 32, 34, 43, 57, 64, 67, 69, 70, 71, 73, 74, 77, 78, 81, 83, 86, 93, 98, 101-106, 114, 118, 129, 131, 136, 138, 141
San Antonio River 18, 44, 54, 76, 78, 81, 83, *96, 143*
San Diego, Texas 113, 114
Sandusky, W.H. 85
San Felipe Consultation 64, 71, 89
San Jacinto, Battle of 3, 7, 9, *10, 11*, 21, 58, 66, 74, 77, 78, 84, 86, 90, 91, 92, 98, 118, 122, 133
San Jacinto River 7, 9
San José y San Miguel de Aguayo Mission 15, *16*
San Marcos River 30
San Patricio 25, *33*, 34, 37, 38, *39*, 57, 66, 67, 70, 73, 77, 78, 80, 84, 85, 86, 87, 95, 96, 113, 128, 129
San Patricio Battalion 66
San Patricio, Battle of 11, 66
San Patricio Cemetery 34
San Patricio Colony 29, 32, 35-40, 44, 46, 47, 57, 64, 66, 67, 70, 73, 74, 76, 77, 79, 107
San Patricio de Hibernia (St. Patrick of Ireland); see San Patricio
San Patricio Rangers 85
Santa Anna, Antonio López de 7, 9, 21, 63, 64, 66, 69, 73, 74, 75, 78, 84, 85, 86, 87, 90, 91
Santa Fe Expedition 101
Santa Gertrudis de Altar (presidio) 17
Santa Margarita Crossing, Nueces River 36
Santos, de los (surname) 84, 96
Saucedo, José Antonio 36
Savannah, Georgia 32
Sayle, Antoine 77
Scanlan, Thomas H. 122
Scotland 1

Scott, Henry 49, *82*, 83
Scott, John 82
Scull, Sally 60
Seale, Bradford 26
Seale, Mary Henry 26
Sea Lion (ship) 43
Sealy, George 123
Secession Convention 103
Secession, Ordinance of 97
Seridan, Enrique 19
Shackelford County 122
Shahan, Benjamin 28
Shahan, Daniel 28
Shahan, Elizabeth 28
Shahan, William P. 28
Shamrock Hose Company 108
Shannon, Andrew 28
Shannon, Robert E. 28
Shannon family 104
Shaw, James B. 134
Shearn, John 122
Sheridan, Enrique; see Enrique Seridan
Sibley's Brigade 98
Sidick, Anthony 76
Sidick, John 76
Siege of Béxar (San Antonio) 70
Sims, Richard 18
Sinnot, John 43
Sinton 38
Sister Angela 128
Sisters of Mary 128
Sisters of the Holy Ghost *130*, 130-31
Sisters of the Holy Spirit 131
Snider, Mrs. Hallie Fagan 53
Sonora, Mexico 17
South Carolina 26
Southwestern Bell Telephone Company 60
Spain 13, 15, 21, 32
Spindletop *118*, 119-20,
Staggers Point 1, 12, 26, 27
Star of the West (ship) 111
Stevens family 104
Sullivan, James 28
Sullivan City 121
Sweeney (surname) 120
Sweeney, John 37
Swift, Thad 60
Tarrant County 27
Taylor, Zachary 107, 128
Teal, Mrs. Annie Fagan 48, 78, 82
Teal, Peter 78, 81, 82
Temple 129
Test Act 14
Texas capitol at Houston *135*
Texas Confederate Command 119
Texas Horticulturist Society 134
Texas Rangers 80, 101, 116, 137-40
Texas Transportation Company 122
Texas War of Independence 84
The Heroine (ship) 42
"The Placeto" 53
"The United Irishmen" (political movement) 14
Third Congress of the Republic 79
Third Order of St. Francis 112-13
Thomas ranch 84
Thompson, Ben 137
Tinsley, James W. 92
Tir na nOg (The Land of Youth) 49

Tobin, W.C. 138
Tone (surname) 3
Trammel, Burke 74
Travis, William Barret 74
Trinity Bay 23
Trinity College, Dublin, Ireland 133
Trinity River 19, 27, 28, 117, 120
Twohig, John 101, *102*
Twohig residence *102*
Tynan family 104
Union Pacific Railroad 138
United States 19, 23, 25, 28, 66, 78, 117, 125, 136
University of Dallas 109
University of Dublin 134
University of Edinburgh 133
University of Texas at Austin 103
University of Texas Medical Department *124*
Uprising, Irish, 1798 14, 26, 29, 93, 103
Urrea, José 21, 73, 74, 75, 84, 91, 95
Usher, Patrick 133
Uvalde County 137
Vaquero of the Brush Country, A, by J. Frank Dobie 82
Valera, Ramón 86, 87, 96
Valverde, Battle of 98
Vara, Rafael de la 75, 96
Vásquez, Rafael 86, 87, 96
Viaje de Indios 18
Victoria 26, 34, 52, 55, 64, 67, 70, 75, 77, 79, 82, 83, 84, 85, 89-94, *90*, 93, 95, 108, 131
Victoria County 38
Vidaurri y Borrego, José 43
Viesca, Agustín 63, 64
Vikings 3
Villa de Santisima Trinidad de Salcedo 19
Vincentian Fathers 109
Vinegar Hill, Battle of 29
Virginia 19, 119, 127
Waco 130, 142
Wales 1
Ward, Thomas W. 134
Ward, William B. 74, 75, 95, 135
Ward County 121
Washington, George 142
Washington-on-the-Brazos 64
Washington, D.C. 134
Watson, William 134
Watts, Mrs. H.O. 83-84
Webb County 121
West Indies 13
Westover, Ira 66, 70, 75
Wharton, William A. 23
Whelan, Dennis, family 109
Whelan, Henry 87
Whelan, Michael *86*, 87
Whelan family 112
Wildcat (ship) 43
William of Orange 13
Williams, John 70
Wise County 27
Woll, Adrian 101, 138
Woodworth, Mary Frances Power, residence *46*
Yucatán 18
Zacatecas 16, 64